# KEEP your COOL

First published in 2013 by Franklin Watts

Text © Dr Aaron Balick 2013
Illustrations and design © Franklin Watts 2013
Franklin Watts
338 Euston Road
London NW1 3BH

Franklin Watts Australia
Level 17/207 Kent Street
Sydney, NSW 2000

Editor: Paul Rockett
Design: Matt Lilly
Illustrator: Clotilde Szymanski

Dewey number: 155.9'042

ISBN: 978 1 4451 1509 2

Printed in China

Franklin Watts is a division of Hachette Children's Books,
an Hachette UK company.

www.hachette.co.uk

# KEEP your COOL

# HOW TO DEAL WITH LIFE'S WORRIES AND STRESS

## Dr Aaron Balick

**W**

# FRANKLIN WATTS
LONDON • SYDNEY

# CONTENTS

## INTRODUCTION

6    A guide to keeping cool

7    You, your perceptions and the world

## ABOUT YOU

10    Knowing yourself better

12    Being your best

14    How you see yourself

16    Getting a grip

18    Feeling stuck?

20    How you talk to yourself

22    Being nasty to yourself

24    Keeping it real

*What's my story?*

## LIFE AT HOME

26    Families

28    Family rows

30    Family time and family meetings

32    Your own space

34    Too stressed to sleep!

36    Managing your time

38    When big stuff comes up in families

40    Big family change

*It's all about attitude!*

## SCHOOL LIFE

42  Making it good
44  Being at school
46  Study skills
48  Exams
50  After school activities

*Be respectful!*

## FRIENDS, FRENEMIES AND ENEMIES

52  Good friends
54  Bullying
58  Cyberbullying
60  More than friends
62  Sexuality and gender is for everyone
66  Feeling frisky
68  Being you and being you with them

## MODERN LIFE

*We're connected!*

70  Being connected
72  The Social Network
74  Your future
76  NOW THAT YOU'RE COOL

77  Glossary
78  Further resources
79  Index

# INTRODUCTION

# A guide to keeping cool

We all lose our cool, worry and get anxious for all sorts of reasons. That's just part of life. The trick is not to work yourself up or to lose your cool more than you really have to. This book will help you to understand yourself better and by doing that you can deal with difficult things without losing your cool.

## Using the book

The best way to work though this book is to understand the main concepts first, and then go to the 'Try it out' exercises to put them to work. Concepts are just ideas about how things work. The ones in this book help you to look at the stuff that happens in your life in a new way. The first concept you encounter is about perceptions — this just means the unique way in which you see the world.

*Hmmmmm, that meditation exercise on page 21 would be great to try before my exams.*

The exercises are designed to get you to think in a certain way, not just to solve a single problem. So, see if you can use the tricks you learn in one exercise for lots of different areas in your life.

Some of the exercises may seem a bit weird, but trust me, once you get going you'll see why they work. There's also lots of extra information in the 'Keep cool' sections (see below for an example).

## You can't do it all on your own*

Throughout this book you'll be learning some tricks to help you keep cool, deal with stress and achieve your goals. Still, it's important to know that it almost always helps to talk through your problems with somebody that you trust. You may need to think hard about who that might be.

You might have different trusted people for different sorts of problems. Maybe a parent will work for some stuff but not for others. It's good to keep a mental list of your top trusted people and between them you should be able to talk about anything.

* There are some good tips on page 38 for how to identify the kind of person you might want to talk to.

# You, your perceptions and the world

Throughout this book we will be looking at how to keep cool in all the major areas of your life. But first it's important to understand that the way you respond to things that happen to you is the key to making changes for the better.

The concepts in this introduction will help to show you that while you can't control the world, you can choose how you react to it. Most people think there is a direct relationship between themselves and the world. Guess what? There isn't! It's just not true!

It really works like this:

> You → your perceptions → the world

## Perceptions

Your perceptions are like the sunglasses through which you see the world — the way your glasses are coloured totally affect the way you experience the world. You know the expression 'seeing the world through rose-tinted spectacles'? That's an optimistic way of looking at the world. What colour would you choose for a pessimistic way of looking at the world? I think crap-coloured glasses is a pretty good description of that.

In this book you will be thinking about three main things that impact on your perceptions:

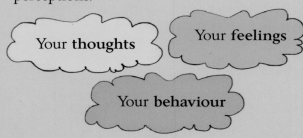

> Your **thoughts**
>
> Your **feelings**
>
> Your **behaviour**

By knowing the difference between your thoughts, feelings and behaviour and how they interact with each other, you can learn how to make better choices and feel cooler in your life.

# Thoughts, feelings and behaviour

Think about a really big thing that has happened to you in your life and try to remember it in detail.

## What happened?

You'll probably find that lots of thoughts and feelings overlap with each other, but try to notice the difference between something like 'I thought something terrible would happen' (a **thought**) and 'I was worried' (a **feeling**). Then, what did you do? Maybe, 'I ran away' (a **behaviour**).

## See the difference?

By working out the difference between a thought, a feeling and behaviour you are better able to understand and react to both big and small things that happen in your life.

# Action!

When something happens to you (in this book we call that an action), you will have thoughts and feelings about it. What you DO in response to that (your behaviour) totally depends on your thoughts and your feelings.

That means there's a really important space between what happens to you and how you respond to that action with your thoughts, feelings and behaviour.

While you can't change an action (because it's just something that happens TO you), you CAN change your thoughts. Since your thoughts affect your feelings, they both matter a whole lot in how you respond to an action.

Get it?

Thoughts

Behaviour

Feelings

Okay, I get that there's a difference between thoughts, feelings and behaviour, but I don't see how that helps me in the real world!

Ritchie

Good point! Let's say Ritchie is in class when his teacher asks, 'Who wants to be the leader of a really exciting class project?'

The action here is the teacher asking for a volunteer. Now it's up to Ritchie to respond to his perceptions about the action, which is all about his thoughts and feelings*.

## Ritchie 1

**Thoughts:** I'm no good at being a leader...

**Feelings:** Sad, shy, low self-esteem.

**Behaviour:** Head and shoulders stooped, sad face, hands in pockets.

**Result:** Someone else is appointed leader

## Ritchie 2

**Thoughts:** It'll be a challenge, but I think I'm up for it!

**Feelings:** A little nervous, a little scared, but mostly excited.

**Behaviour:** Puts up his hand.

**Result:** Teacher appoints him leader

Can you see how that space between you and the world makes such a big difference? By getting to know how you think about the world, and making changes when necessary, you can change the actual results of your life!

## So...

By getting a handle on your thoughts and feelings you can make better choices about how to respond (behave) when things happen in your life (actions). Now that you understand that, let's apply it to the BIG areas of your life...

> * Another way of thinking about it would be to ask what colour glasses might Ritchie wear, and how might that affect his thoughts, feelings and behaviour?

# Knowing yourself better

Way back in ancient Greece there was a place called the Temple of Delphi where people used to go to see an oracle who would tell them their future.

At the front of this temple was a sign that read, 'Know yourself'. Now, the oracle never told the future very clearly. It was always told like a puzzle that had to be worked out. The better you knew yourself, the better you were at understanding the message. If you didn't know yourself at all, you'd only hear what you wanted to hear and the message would be of no help.

That ancient advice holds as much value today as it did way back then. By knowing yourself, you can direct your future much better than if you don't.

## How well do you know yourself?

It may seem like an odd question, but it's an important one. Sure, you know lots of stuff about you, but think on all levels, especially about your thoughts and feelings. What do you really know?

*Who am I... really?*

## TRY IT OUT  Keeping a journal

One of the best ways to get to know yourself is to keep a journal or a diary. This is your private place to write down your thoughts and your feelings about stuff that's going on in your life. Your journal is just for you, so make sure you hide it away in a good place.

Getting your thoughts and feelings out of your head and onto paper can really give you a new perspective on your life. Feel free to write whatever you want in your journal; don't censor it. This is a place to be completely honest with yourself.

# Personality

We've all got different parts to our personalities and we all act differently depending on what's happening to us. Think of how differently you act at school, with your parents, with your friends or with a bunch of people you don't know. You're still the same person, you're just using different parts of your personality.

Your personality is not one single thing; it's a combination of lots of different parts of yourself that change over time. You'll have a way of being that is more comfortable and familiar to you, and other ways of being that you may find a bit more difficult. It's a bit like handedness: you can use both hands pretty well, but generally you have a preference for being left-handed or right-handed.

Think of the personalities of the people in your life. How are you like them and how are you different? There is nothing 'right' or 'wrong' about your personality; it is just different. That's a good thing. If we were all the same, how boring would that be? It would be like living in a zombie world!

Keeping cool isn't about changing your personality (that's yours to keep and enjoy!). The trick is to get to know your personality so you can be in the world in the best possible way — your OWN way.

*Man, get a personality!*

## TRY IT OUT

## Personality inventory

In your journal, write down some words that best describe your personality. I'll start you off with some of my own, but you should choose those that work for you and add lots more.

happy  sad  shy  sensitive funny  worried  outgoing  intense people person  weird  nice a bit prickly...

Once you've written a load of words down, see if you can draw your personality. Create a character who expresses the words that you have written down.

### Get creative!

Try it with paints, markers, crayons or even making a collage out of cut out bits in magazines.

This can be a fun exercise to do with friends too. You can mix up all your drawings and see if your friends can guess who is who. Do they see you as you see yourself?

# Being your best

Your thoughts, feelings and behaviour are super important, and they are what we'll be looking at mostly in this book. Still, there's a lot more to you than just those, and it's best to keep on top of the other things too. These sorts of things include:

**Emotional:** how you feel about other people, how you feel about things and respond to events.

**Physical:** how to look after your body (nutrition, exercise, sleep, etc).

**Mental:** how to look after your thinking (creativity, school work, how you think about the world, how you think other people think, etc).

**Social:** your relationships with others.

**Spiritual:** what you believe about the big things, such as the meaning of life and the universe.

In order for each of these things to be top notch, they need to be in some degree of balance. For example, if you are physically tired, it's hard to concentrate (bad for mental), it can put you in a bad mood (bad for emotional) and then you can get ratty with your friends (bad for social), so everything is tied together.

This approach is called **holistic**, which means covering all aspects of your life.

Getting these things sorted may seem a bit like juggling, but by keeping your eyes on the balls it'll feel less like juggling and more like balancing.

# Topping up on all levels

Below are some suggestions for ways to keep on top of each of these areas, but I am sure you can come up with more:

**Physical:** getting lots of exercise and spending time outdoors, eating well and laying off too much caffeine and sugar, and getting lots of sleep.

**Mental:** keeping your mind active by reading books and taking on difficult challenges and puzzles.

**Emotional:** learning to accept your feelings, talking things through with people you trust, writing in your journal.

**Social:** trying to keep good, honest relationships with others, being respectful, listening to others and being listened to.

**Spiritual:** asking important questions about the world and thinking hard about the answers you get.

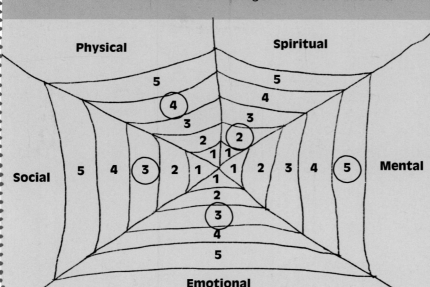

**TRY IT OUT**

## 'Being my best' spider diagram

A spider diagram is a great way to see where you stand in relation to these categories. It looks like this:

Physical    Spiritual

Social    Mental

Emotional

Make a diagram like this in your journal. Score yourself honestly on how well you're doing on each of these categories, reaching out to the edge with a five if you're doing well in that area or closer to the centre at a one or two if you feel that category needs more work. Then you'll know what you need to handle more urgently, and what you can leave be for a while.

# How you see yourself

We all have a **self-image**. You've probably heard of words like 'self-esteem' and 'self-worth' which are all about how you value yourself. Self-image covers all these things, and it's handy because it's about how you see yourself; but it is also the way you imagine other people see you.

Believe it or not we rarely see ourselves clearly. Just think of how you look to yourself in the mirror when you're in a bad mood compared to when you're feeling great. Maybe just four hours have passed from one mood to the other, but you can move from ugly to pretty hot that quickly*.

This is all about that space between you and the world. The way you see yourself makes up a lot of the way you see things out in the world: it's your self-image that colours your glasses.

Your self-image is made up of all the stories you have heard about yourself from a really young age.

AGE 12 ONWARDS
AGES 8 TO 12
AGES 5 TO 8
AGES 2 TO 5
AGES 0 TO 2

## Finding the truth

When Leslie was five years old her mother said to her, 'You'll never be good at maths; no one in our family is ever good at maths!' Leslie believed this for years, and indeed did terribly in maths all through school. Later, she decided she wanted to be an aviation engineer, and needed maths GCSEs and A-levels to do that. She worked really hard to get rid of that 'bad-at-maths' idea, studied tons and got the grades she needed. Her self-image of being bad at maths was clearly untrue.

Like Leslie, you probably have some bad chapters in the story of your self-image. This book will help you to learn what they are so you can change them.

*Already you can see the relationship between self-image and body-image. It's generally not that you look bad; it's that you feel you look bad.

# What you believe is what you see

I won't fool you, it's hard work to change your self-image, but if you're up for it you can. You start by wondering: are all the things I believe about myself true?

At the very bottom of your self-image is an idea that fits into a tiny sentence. These are called **core beliefs** and you can have them about yourself, other people and the world. Most of us have a few of these and they can be positive or negative.

A positive core belief about yourself would be something like 'I'm pretty OK' or 'People like me.' Sadly lots of us have negative core beliefs like 'I'm not good enough' or 'Nobody likes me.'

Core beliefs about others include 'I can trust other people' or 'People always let me down' while core beliefs about the world can be things like 'The world is full of opportunity' or 'The world is a scary and lonely place.'

All of your core beliefs together contribute to how you feel about yourself.

## Your own jar of coins

A cool way to think about your self-image is to imagine a glass jar that you keep golden coins in. Every golden coin is like an investment in yourself. When you do things you are proud of it's like you are putting golden coins in that jar. When your jar looks full, you feel good about yourself; when the jar looks empty you tend not to feel so good.

When you have a low self-image it doesn't necessarily mean there aren't enough coins in your jar, it's that you don't notice that they're even in there.

By thinking about things in your life that you are proud of and making sure that they turn into coins in your jar, you can improve your self-image!

Throughout this book we'll be thinking about how you can put coins in your jar by doing and thinking about things you're proud of, but also about how to notice the coins that are already there.

# Getting a grip

Lots of your core beliefs can be outdated and resistant to new facts about yourself, other people and the world. If you don't want to be limited by your core beliefs, then it's good to know it's possible to change them.

It's as easy as ABC!

By learning your ABCs, you'll learn how to respond to things better in your life so you don't get so worked up (stressed), so worked down (depressed), or so worked sideways (anxious). By using these tools, you can take better control of your life, and even improve how things turn out!

Now we're going to use everything you've learned so far and put it into an easy to understand formula – and don't worry it's not real maths!

## $A + B = C$

Where...

### A = Action
This is the thing that happens out in the world and is outside your control. In Ritchie's case (page 9) it was his teacher asking for volunteers. Her asking was the A.

### B = Beliefs
This is what you believe about the thing that's happened. Beliefs exist in that 'my perceptions' space between you and the world. Ritchie's wondering whether or not he was up for the challenge offered by his teacher was his B.

### C = Consequence
The consequence is the thing that happens as a result of your beliefs about the action. Think of Ritchie's two consequences, of being appointed leader or not: that's his C.

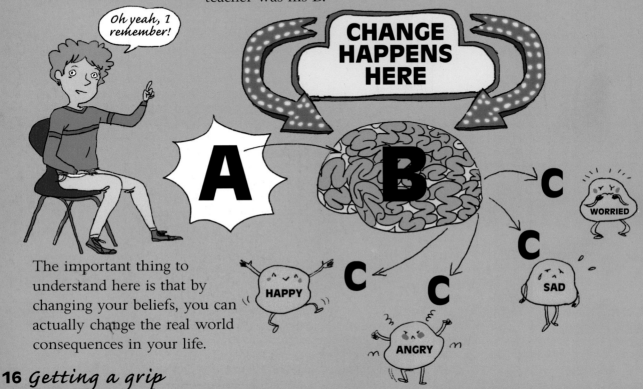

*Oh yeah, 1 remember!*

CHANGE HAPPENS HERE

**A** **B** **C** **C** **C** **C**

WORRIED  HAPPY  SAD  ANGRY

The important thing to understand here is that by changing your beliefs, you can actually change the real world consequences in your life.

**I'm going to say this again because it is SO important:**

If you can change your **beliefs** about yourself in response to the **actions** that happen in your world, you can change how things actually happen in your life.
IT'S ONE OF LIFE'S GREAT SECRETS!

*Oh, I get it!*

The more you get to know yourself, the way you think, feel and believe, the better you'll be able to respond to the **As** in your life and have better **Cs**. Throughout this book we'll be looking at a variety of different ways to change your **Bs** to help you feel better and get better **Cs**.

Can you think of a time when one of your beliefs affected the way something turned out in your life?

BELIEFS

**TRY IT OUT**

## Putting it to work

Think of a time when something didn't work out very well for you.
Describe it in your journal.

*What belief may have got in the way of a better outcome?*
*Can you imagine what might have happened if you had a different belief?*
*How might it have changed your C?*

Now think of something that's coming up in your life. What beliefs do you already have about that event? Do you think you might be able to change some of them and have a better consequence?

# Feeling stuck?

Have you ever heard the expression 'self-fulfilling prophecy'? It's when people get exactly what they expect to get. If you expect to fail at something, you are more likely to fail — but if you expect to succeed, you are more likely to do just that (it also helps not to be so frightened of failure*).

Self-fulfilling prophecies happen because you get stuck into **good loops** and **bad loops**. In a bad loop you respond to an A (action) with a negative B (belief) which is likely to give you a bad C (consequence). That consequence then proves your negative belief, and sets you up for more negative beliefs, and so on, *ad nauseum***. Now that's what I call a bad loop or what some people call a **vicious cycle**.

Now, let's see how this works in practice.

Take the story of Julie. She's new to her school, and gets invited to a party for the first time. The thing is, because she doesn't know anybody she's feeling a bit shy and isn't sure she can face going. Let's see how things work out in a negative loop and then a positive one:

**Thoughts:** negative, failure-based, stressing weaknesses and fears

**Feelings:** depressed, frightened, anxious, looking backward

**Behaviour:** doesn't confront fears, doesn't take risks, stays isolated

**Consequence:** negative, feels lonely, more withdrawn

## Bad loop

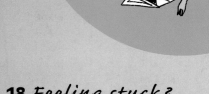

A. Julie gets invited to a party

B. Thinks nobody will like her

C. Feels shy and sad

D. Decides not to go

E. Doesn't get invited to the next party

* See page 74 for more on seeing failure differently.

**Ad nauseum** is Latin for 'until you feel like you're going to throw up' — try that phrase in your next piece of homework.

A good loop is just the opposite of a bad one. If you respond to that very same action with a more helpful thought, you change not only THAT consequence, but set up a whole new good loop: some people call this a **virtuous cycle**.

## Good loop

A. Julie gets invited to a party

B. Thinks it might be an opportunity to make friends

C. Feels shy, but also excited

D. Goes to the party and enjoys herself

E. Makes friends and gets invited to more parties

**Thoughts:** positive, acknowledge success, balanced and recognise strengths

**Feelings:** shy but excited, hopeful, looking forward

**Behaviour** confronts fear, takes a risk, reaches out

**Consequences:** positive, feels included, makes friends

Can you see how the B makes all the difference? Changing your B doesn't mean you won't be scared or feel shy, it just means you're more likely to do it IN SPITE OF your nervous feelings. The more you do it, the better you get at it.

**KEEP COOL**

## Change the playlist!

The beliefs and the stories we have about ourselves are a bit like a playlist on an MP3 player that keeps going over and over and over *ad nauseum*\*. Don't you get tired of the same old playlist? Of course you do, and that's why you change it.

Now, you can't re-invent yourself the way you can make a whole new playlist, but you can listen closely to each of the tracks on your playlist and think, 'You know what? This one doesn't work anymore. I'm going to choose a new track.'

Changing that track is the first step to changing the beliefs that keep you in a bad loop.

\* Remember that?

# How you talk to yourself

If you've got a tired old playlist looping in your head, listen in carefully. The tracks on it are made up of your Bs and if you want to change them you have to get the measure of them first.

*Talking to myself???*

Instead of being like songs, our Bs tend to be found in the way we talk to ourselves.

Yes. We all do it; in fact, we talk to ourselves most of the time about most everything! In fact, it's called **automatic thinking** – most of the time we don't even know we're doing it. It's like there's a little robot in us feeding us lines that do us no good!*

Imagine how much it affects you if this robot is talking in your ears all the time?

*You're walking to school...*

*Look who's that?*

*Oh! it's Jo! I hope she didn't see me...*

Your automatic thoughts are very powerful because:

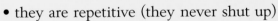

- they are repetitive (they never shut up)
- they feel like the truth, even when lots of the time they are not
- you listen to them and make decisions based on them
- you believe what they say about you
- they make up your Bs and by doing that they affect your Cs
- you're so used to talking to yourself that you hardly notice you're doing it

Stop right now for just 30 seconds. Can you hear yourself saying anything to yourself? What sort of things are you saying?

*Don't confuse automatic thinking with what some people call your 'inner voice'. By learning to quiet down and control your automatic thinking, you'll be more conscious of your inner voice which tends to tell you stuff about yourself you need to know.

# Mindfulness

A great way to get a sense of your automatic thoughts is to be mindful of them. **Mindfulness** is about being non-judgementally aware of yourself at any given moment. That means you just notice what's happening without making any decisions about whether it's right or wrong: just noticing. It's a bit like watching yourself from a distance.

It's really tough to be mindful when you're reacting to something big in your life and sometimes you just have to try to be mindful about it afterwards. By developing this skill, you can learn to respond to things better.

## TRY IT OUT

## Awareness meditation

By learning to be mindful you become aware of what's going on inside you: your feelings, your thoughts, the way your body feels etc. You'd be surprised how little most people know about what's happening to them in any moment!

**1** Find a quiet and comfortable place to sit* where you won't be interrupted. Sitting cross-legged on a cushion is a good way to do it.

**2** Set an alarm for 10 minutes, but make sure the alarm sound is gentle and not jarring.

**3** Close your eyes and breathe deeply, be in the present moment, and keep your mind completely open.

**4** Let your mind wander and just notice your thoughts, memories or fantasies – just notice them and let them go without judging them.

**5** It can help to think of your thoughts and feelings like bubbles floating across your field of vision. Just notice what is inside one until the next one comes along.

**6** At the end of the meditation open your eyes, take a deep breath and get on with your day.

You'll probably be surprised how many thoughts you have, and you'll learn quickly how filled up your brain becomes. By getting a sense of how mindfulness works, you'll be able to slow down, feel less stressed and get less hung up on all that thinking.

*On page 33 you'll learn how to make a Zen space, which is the perfect place to do something like this.

# Being nasty to yourself

Automatic thinking covers all the thoughts you have at any given moment. When automatic thoughts are negative, we call it **negative self-talk**. Negative self-talk can be really destructive because it's so constant and repetitive.

It's important to identify your negative self-talk. Most people are so used to theirs that they hardly notice it: but that doesn't mean it's not bad news.

Negative self-talk:

- Is all about the downers, really pessimistic and hopeless.
- In negative self-talk something isn't 'could have been better' but rather 'really awful'.
- It's stubborn, staying negative even if the facts say something different.
- It tries to predict the future as something that is going to be totally awful.

> I look really crap today!
>
> I'm boring
>
> I'm no good
>
> I just made a fool out of myself
>
> People don't like me

## Down at the bottom

Can you guess what's at the bottom of your negative self-talk? That's right! Your negative **core beliefs**! The negative self-talk is the way your negative core beliefs get into your head.

If you have a core belief that says, 'I'm no good', you will have negative self-talk that matches that. For example, you may go into your first day at a new school, thinking, 'This is going to suck. What's the point? I'll never make any friends... .'

The worst thing about negative self-talk is that it just doesn't listen to reason! For example, if you always say to yourself, 'I'm really ugly' and somebody else says, 'You look really great today!' you might say, 'Oh, that's because the light is so bad in here!' or, 'You're just being nice,' or, 'You must be crazy!'

# How aware are you of your negative self-talk?

Think of a time that you felt really bad about yourself, like maybe embarrassed, or ashamed. Can you remember what you might have said to yourself? Did it make you feel worse?

Negative self-talk doesn't do you any favours. While we can't get rid of our negative self-talk completely (it's just part of being human), we can quiet it down so it doesn't get in our way so much.

I like to think of my negative self-talk like a monster that hangs around my head trying to convince me how bad everything is.

This is what I imagine that monster to look like.

## TRY IT OUT
## Your negative self-talk monster

Did you know that drawing, painting or even writing out your bad feelings can make you feel better? It's called externalisation: that's what you do when you take the nasty feelings you have inside, and put them outside*.

You can do this with your negative thought monster. What do you think it looks like? Get out a bunch of pens, crayons, markers, whatever, and draw the nastiest negative self-talk monster you can – big fangs, nasty eyes, whatever. Get a really good sense of what it looks like.

Now imagine what your monster would look like if you were able to really beat it up, to tear it apart piece by piece, to make it so it couldn't get into your head and talk you down anymore. Now draw that one. Pretty pathetic, huh? Let's try and make it stay that way.

* That's why one of the first things I asked you to do was get a journal or diary. It's great for externalising your nasty feelings. Have you got yours yet?

# Keeping it real

Your negative self-talk monster isn't very realistic. It has its own ideas about you and never listens to **evidence** against those ideas. In psychology this is called **filtering**. Filtering explains why some of the coins in your jar are invisible (see page 15). When you filter out stuff that doesn't match the story your monster tells you, it's like making the coins that are there invisible.

*Does my bum look big in this?*

*YES, YES, YES! Your bum looks HUGE!*

*No! I think you look great!*

Carrie has a self-talk monster that always tells her that she's fat and ugly: but she's not!

Whenever Carrie gets a compliment she somehow makes it so it doesn't matter*. That's filtering for you! If the compliment doesn't fit her story, she won't believe it (and the coins can't appear in her jar).

By learning to hear the evidence and to stop filtering, Carrie can change her story about herself, and you can do the same.

# How to find the evidence

Evidence is the best weapon against a negative self-talk monster. When you find yourself under attack by yours, take a time-out and ask some questions like these:

*Evidence questions*

*1. Where is the evidence that what I'm thinking is true?*

*2. Is there any evidence pointing the other way?*

*3. Am I basing my thoughts on all the available information?*

*4. Am I thinking in 'black and white' — is there a grey zone?*

*5. Am I blaming myself for something that may not be entirely my fault?*

*6. Am I upset because I expect myself to be perfect (when we all make mistakes)?*

*7. Am I overestimating the awfulness of what's happened or is going to happen?*

*8. Am I putting too much importance on this one thing?*

By REALLY answering these questions, you are likely to feel much better about the situation and make your monster smaller.

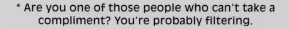
\* Are you one of those people who can't take a compliment? You're probably filtering.

Let's see how this works with Zack who had to do a presentation at school. When it was over he got the following feedback:

- his teacher gave him a B+
- his teacher said he spoke too fast, and should slow down next time
- all the students applauded when he finished
- his mates came up to him afterwards and said 'well done!'
- someone in class asked for his help on their presentation.

But when Zack went home:

How did your presentation go?

The teacher said I spoke too fast.

Hee, hee!

Can you see that Zack filtered out all the good stuff to stick to his monster's idea that it was no good? How might he feel if he'd gone through all the evidence?

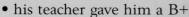

## Sorting through the evidence

Try testing the evidence about something in your life that you feel bad about. In your journal, draw out a table like the one Zack completed below.

| Date | Event | Negative self-talk | Evidence for and against* | Your thoughts after the evidence |
|------|-------|-------------------|---------------------------|----------------------------------|
| Monday | Class presentation | I'm no good; I'm not smart enough; I'm scared of presenting; I don't know anything. | Teacher said I spoke too fast; I got a good grade; my friends really liked it; Julie asked me for help on hers (and she wouldn't have if mine was so bad). | I did pretty well, and will remember to speak more slowly next time. |

By checking the evidence Zack is able to see that in fact he did really well. Instead of getting hung up on 'talking too fast' he can take it as a learning point so he'll be able to do even better next time.

## It's starting to make sense

When you get to understand your core beliefs and the thoughts they produce, you're better able to challenge them with evidence and develop more helpful ways of thinking. This will increase your self-image and help you keep your cool in a whole variety of situations.

* Use the evidence questions on the previous page to help you with this section.

# Families

You spend a whole lot of your time at home, so it's really important to keep your home life as cool as possible. Sometimes families can be tough because parents and siblings can be hard to get on with. But families can also be our biggest support.

Families come in all shapes and sizes; you may be an only child or have loads of siblings; maybe both your parents are at home or just one; you may live in one house or travel between two; maybe you've got step-parents, step-siblings, half-siblings, live with your grandparents; maybe you are brought up in a care home, or with foster parents... the possibilities are endless!

In this book, I use the word 'family' in the broadest way — think of it just as those people you live with and spend the most time with.

## TRY IT OUT
## What's your family's story?

In your journal, write down the story of your family.
Tell the story from your perspective; what it's like to be YOU in your family.
If you feel artistic, you might want to illustrate your story.

You might see if other members of your family want to participate by writing their stories too. Then pick a time to sit together and tell your stories. You might be surprised what you learn and it's a great way to get to know each other better.

my family

Think: Who are the main characters? Would you include the dog? Or maybe your uncle? How do the different characters interact with each other? What are the big events that have happened in your family? How are you as a family unit now?

# Jars of coins are for families too

Remember your jar of coins (page 15)? Now it's time to think about that again, but this time with your family. Everybody in your family has their own jar and the health of your family as a whole is sort of like a giant family jar that everyone shares.

Can you think of ways to keep your family jars topped up?
Here are some suggestions:

1. Make the time to listen and talk to each other.
2. Be sure to thank and appreciate each other.
3. Support each other's accomplishments both in and outside the family.
4. Always treat each other with respect.

---

TRY IT OUT

## Family relationship map

### How do you feel you get on with the different members of your family?

In your journal, draw a plan of your family with yourself in the middle. Then, draw lines connecting you to your family members using different coloured pens. The colours represent different aspects of your relationships. You could use blue to show trust, green for communication and red for conflict. The thicker the line the more there is of this aspect in your relationship. For example, make the blue lines thicker to show where there is a lot of trust with this person, and thinner to show when there is not so much trust.

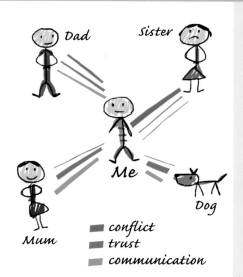

Dad    Sister

Me

Mum    Dog

conflict
trust
communication

This map can help you to understand how you fit in with your family. You could even have your whole family do a map and compare them. You can then find out where the problems are and begin to start fixing them through communication and cooperation.

If you found a really thick red line between you and a member of your family it can help to talk about it with that person. If that feels too scary, it can help to have another person there to help (someone you've got thick green and blue lines with).

# Family rows

Did you know that most **conflict** in families is actually pretty normal? Conflict happens simply because different people have different expectations. In families, since everyone lives so close to each other those expectations rub against each other a lot.

Conflict itself isn't a problem; it's how you deal with it that really matters. Here are two common but not-so-good ways lots of families deal with it:

1. Lots of screaming and shouting (that goes nowhere).

2. Lots of quietly angry people steaming up inside like pressure cookers.

The key to keeping it cool at home is through **trust** and **communication** so conflict can be dealt with better. That means calmly working through conflict and talking about it. By learning to deal with conflict WELL, we don't have to scream and yell or sweep it under the carpet*.

## TRY IT OUT — Active listening

Active listening is a great tool for dealing with any conflict. It is a simple way to make sure you are actually listening to the other person and it lets the other person KNOW you're really listening back:

**1** Keep eye contact by facing the person who is speaking.

**2** Focus your attention on the speaker and make an effort to understand from their perspective.

**3** Indicate that you are listening by saying, 'Uh huh' or 'I see' or 'Please explain that again.'

> I see.

**4** Repeat back what you understood and let them correct you if you've got something wrong.

**5** Don't be in a rush to tell your thoughts. Make sure you've understood their side first.

**6** Encourage them to do the same.

---

* Sometimes feelings are too 'hot' to discuss in a family, especially when things are really tough and out of control. In those cases think about who you might be able to talk to outside your immediate family — perhaps a teacher, an aunt or an uncle.

# Timing

Timing is crucial when it comes to sorting conflict. Sometimes the biggest mistake people make is trying to sort out conflicts while feelings are HOT. It's not a good idea! Wait until things cool down. Don't start a conversation about conflict when you or the other person is really angry or upset.

If you've got a conflict you want to fix, the best time to do it is when:

- the person you want to speak to is calm
- when that person isn't distracted
- when there is time to see it through (so not 15 minutes before you have to be somewhere).

Set a time in advance by saying, something like, 'I want to have a talk with you. Can we take some time to do it this afternoon, when we won't have any interruptions?'

Probably not the best time to have a heart-to-heart.

Resolve conflict by doing your best to avoid winding people up and making them defensive.

- Don't be blaming. Try using 'I' language (see below).
- Listen to the other person's side of the story by using your active listening skills. Try not to raise your voice!
- Be prepared to compromise and meet the other person half-way.

## Using 'I' language

Starting a conversation with 'You really annoyed me when...' or 'You're in trouble mate' is a sure way to get conflict going again. Starting with 'You' followed by blame, puts the other person on the spot, making them defensive. Use 'I' language instead.

Saying, 'I feel hurt when you compare me to my sister,' is softer than saying, 'You make me feel angry when you compare me to my sister!' You'll get a better response with 'I' language.

By using 'I' language you take responsibility for your feelings and stop blaming others.
If both parties use 'I' language, it can make dealing with conflict much easier.

# Family time and family meetings

With everyone caught up in work, school or home life, a family can seem like just the people you live alongside. By organising family time at least once a week (and more if you can) you can be a family that hang out together, get to know and support each other better.

Family time is about enjoying each other's company:

IT SHOULDN'T BE A CHORE!

To make good family time:

• the time and place is agreed in advance
• for this bit of time, it's 'family first'
• it should be fun and interesting for everyone, and not a drag
• everyone makes a commitment to be a part of it.

Each family time is arranged by a 'planner' and each member of the family takes their turn as planner. Mix it up. One day someone can prepare a special meal, another day someone may organise a game or go somewhere special. While everyone agrees the time that the family should meet, it's the planner's responsibility to make things happen.

Still, there are two rules to work by.

1. No distractions: that means TVs, game consoles, mobile phones and all other pinging things are turned off (and this goes for parents too!).*
2. Make sure it's an activity which everyone can enjoy.

Having regular family time can reduce conflict by increasing your communication and trust with each other. Try comparing the first family relationship map you made and then do another one after a month of family activities. Has it changed?

* Of course if you are playing a computer game as a family or watching a DVD, you'll need those devices, but try not to have all your family time in front of the TV!

# Family business

Family meetings are different from family time. They're a bit more serious because they're about doing the 'business' of being a family, which includes scheduling family time.

Family meetings are a time to share news, let people know about events (like a school play, sports event or your local garage band's gig). Any major news that affects the family is discussed.

If it's a small family (even if it's just two of you), this is something you can do over dinner once a week: but it's still important that it's a 'family meeting' dinner, and not like any other meal.

Each family should adapt these suggestions to suit their needs:

- Meetings should be about once a week and shouldn't really take more than an hour.
- Start with a 'go round' where everybody says what's going on for them.
- Here's a chance to talk about any problems, try to resolve conflicts, and tell good news too.
- Make sure everybody knows what's going on when.
- Organise your family time, and make sure everybody knows who is doing what and when.

FAMILY MEETINGS ARE SERIOUS, BUT THEY DON'T HAVE TO BE A CHORE.

THINK OF A WAY TO ALWAYS MAKE YOURS FUN!

# Your own space

Your home is full of 'shared spaces' where you all meet to eat, watch TV or use the bathroom. The most harmonious household is one where everybody does the best they can to be respectful of shared places. Even so, living at home can be pretty crowded, so having your own personal space is important, even if it is just a small part of a shared room.

Your space should be a 'cool' zone. As much as possible try to keep it stress free by avoiding clutter and mess. It also helps to surround yourself with things that make you feel good, like posters of cool places or things you have that remind you of good times.

Your space should be a place where you can go to and feel like 'you' — so all the distractions of the day can melt away.

## Feng Shui

One way to think about your space is through Feng Shui, which is an ancient Chinese tradition that teaches how to make the spaces around you more beneficial for your life.

Some Feng Shui tips include:

- getting rid of clutter so you have a fresh, airy and energising space around you
- using colours that suit the mood you want to have in your room
- making sure there is fresh air through open windows and the proper placement of green plants
- strategically placing important symbols around your room to help bring good things into your life.

### TRY IT OUT

## A place for everything

Decorate your space in a way that reflects who you are and what you like.

Ask yourself:

*What is important to me?*

*What inspires me?*

*What makes me happy?*

Cool!

*What colours do I like?*

*What reminds me how to be a better person?*

By decorating your area with these sorts of things you'll find that it helps you remember to feel good and stay cool in your own space.

# Study space, creative space, sleep space

In **psychology** there's a concept called **association**. That's when one thing reminds you of something else: like a desk reminding you of 'work' or a ball making you think of 'play'.

It's important to keep different parts of your space separate (if you can) so you don't mix your 'study' associations with your 'play' associations. Most of all, you want to preserve your 'sleep' associations, so keep the bed area especially clear of anything too exciting*.

Make a desk area especially clear as a message to yourself saying it's 'work time'. For creative stuff, maybe you have another area of your room you can develop. Make sure there's a private place for your journal too. Of course, you can't keep it all perfect, but by being strategic about your space you can make your associations to it top notch!

**TRY IT OUT**

## Creating a Zen space

If you're feeling cramped or upset, and feel you can't find a place of your own, creating a Zen space can be just the thing. Zen is really just about sitting calmly and being you outside the distractions of the world.

Making a Zen space in your room is as simple as putting a cushion on the floor in an uncluttered area. It may help to have a poster there of something calming and natural like the mountains, the beach or a Zen rock garden. Think of Feng Shui and put a symbol there that marks this space out as special.

You can think of this space as a quiet and tranquil zone to chill out, and charge yourself back up. It's where you'll do the meditation exercise you learned on page 21, and the yoga exercise you'll learn later. It's YOUR space to be uniquely you, so make it just right.

* You won't want to hear it, but it's best to keep smartphones, tablets, and TVs off the bed area. They will keep you awake. The only things you should have near your bed is a lamp, alarm clock, a glass of water and maybe a book.

# Too stressed to sleep!

Do you ever get so worked up that you can't sleep? First you can't sleep because you're worrying, then you start to worry about sleeping. Not good!

One of the best things you can do with your worries at night-time is to move them from inside your head to the outside. Time to get out your journal and start *externalising!*

## Write out the worries

When you are feeling overwhelmed at bedtime, get up out of bed and fetch your journal from its secret place. Have a look at your clock and make sure you don't spend any more than 15 or 20 minutes on this.

### The trick here is to:

**1.**
Get it out of your head and onto your paper.

**2.**
Put your worries away for the night so you can rest.

**3.**
Write down anything you don't want to forget for the morning so you can deal with it then.

### Now, LET RIP!

Write down all your worries and get them out of your head (or chest, wherever you feel them) and on to the page.

# Better out than in!

No one but you will ever read your journal, so be honest. The object is just to get the worries out of you, and onto the page. If you're more the arty type, you can draw or sketch your worries too.

Once you've got all that out of your system, turn a page and write a couple of things you don't want to forget, so you can sort them in the morning. Now you've done what you can, you can go back to sleep.

Later, you can come back and subject it to your evidence questions (see page 24) and see how much your level of worrying comes down.

(see page 24)

---

**TRY IT OUT**

## Progressive body relaxation

Sometimes, even after writing down your feelings, you can still feel the stress in your body. In fact, lots of us carry stress in our bodies without even knowing it. Here's a really great exercise to try while you're in bed. You'll probably fall asleep before you even finish it, which is just fine.

Lie down in bed on your back with your arms at your side. In this exercise you squeeze all the stress out of your body one step at a time, while moving towards sleep. You should be breathing nice and deeply the whole time.

**1** Take a big breath in through your nose and squeeze both feet as hard as you can. When you think you've squeezed them as tight as you can, try to do it even harder! Then, release the air in your lungs through you mouth at the same time as letting your feet go. Feel all the stress go from your feet and be replaced by coolness.

**2** Next, do the same thing with your calves, then your knees and thighs all the way up to your hips. Inhale, squeeze, squeeze harder, then release and exhale.

**3** Then move to your hands, then your forearms, upper arms and shoulders; then your tummy and then your chest.

**4** All that's left is your neck and head. Tense up your neck as tightly as you can, and then release it, now scrunch up your face (and be glad no one is looking) and squeeze your tongue against the roof of your mouth, then let it all go.

Now you have squeezed all the stress out of your body and you are totally relaxed from your toes to your head. By doing exercises like this you can wake up refreshed, and be even more ready to deal with the day tomorrow.

# Managing your time

Once you've got your spaces sorted, you'll want to think about how you arrange your time too. We have most of our time sorted for us (between school, after school activities, hobbies etc.), but what about that time that's just for you? It's your time, so it's important you spend it wisely.

## How are you using your time?

There's usually a big difference between how you'd like to use your time, and how you actually use it.

In your journal write out all the activities you do in your personal time. These are things such as time with friends, playing video games, reading, doing homework, watching TV, talking on the phone, being online etc.

Now, make two different pie charts, one on how you generally (HONESTLY!) spend your time, and a second one on how you would most like to be spending your time. Make categories of the way you spend your time like 'being online', 'hanging with friends', 'studying' and 'exercising'.

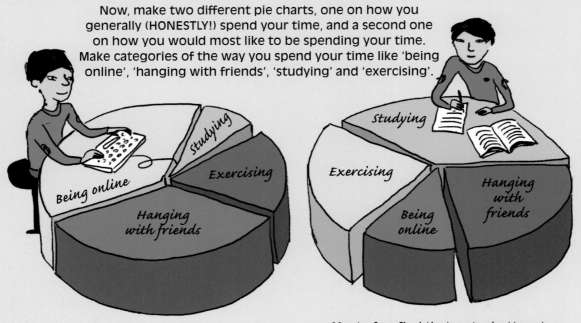

Between the two pies, you may find you need to make lots of adjustments!

Most of us find that we're better at spending our time on stuff we like rather than stuff we don't like – is that what your pie chart looks like?

By managing your time well, you can try to cover both the yucky things and the cool things in the best possible way. When it comes to the yucky things, remember your Bs! Do they really have to be so yucky?* The way we use our time has a lot to do with how stressed out we get, so managing this well is really important.

* For lots of us it's homework and studying that is the most difficult to schedule in. You'll get your basic timekeeping skills here, but we'll come back to homework and exams later on.

# Using positive incentives

A **positive incentive** is the reward you get for putting in hard work, like the A-grade you get when you've studied hard for a test or when you win a medal for a race. While those positive incentives are usually given to us by others, it's also good to know how to give them to yourself too.

When managing your time, it's a good idea to do the difficult stuff first (like chores and homework) and then to follow that up with a positive incentive (like playing a game or watching a favourite TV show).

This helps in two ways:

*1.* You get all the difficult stuff done with and you have something to look forward to.

*2.* When you actually DO the fun stuff, you don't have the difficult stuff hanging over your head.

It takes practice and motivation to do the hard stuff first and save the positive incentive for later, but it's worth it — and not just for now, but for later in life too.

## The Marshmallow Experiment*

Did you know that research shows that people who can put off a **positive incentive** and buckle down first are much more successful FOR THE REST OF THEIR LIVES!

Psychologists know this because they did an experiment with children aged 4–6 called the 'Marshmallow Experiment'. They put a marshmallow in front of a child and said, 'If you don't eat this for 15 minutes, you'll get two marshmallows, but if you eat it before then, you just get the one.'

*What would you do?*

Some of those children ate it straight away, and some saved it for later. You should see how hard it was for them to wait just 15 minutes! When psychologists looked at those same children later in life, the ones who were able to wait did MUCH better in all areas of their lives.

You may think you aren't so good at putting off your positive incentive, but you can learn to do it. It's like a muscle that grows with time and practice, so start working out!

* Officially this was called the 'Stanford Marshmallow Experiment' and was carried out by a psychologist called Walter Mischel in 1972. It's been repeated successfully loads of times since then.

# When big stuff comes up in families

It can be hard enough to deal with the regular everyday stuff that comes up in families, the bickering, the disagreements, the fights and all the rest of it. However, when really big things happen, the small stuff can seem really tiny indeed. So how do you deal with things when the really big stuff comes up?

There may be a time in your life when you have to deal with really upsetting things, like separation or divorce, the death of a pet or even a family member. When these things occur it can feel like life will never get better, like your whole world has fallen apart. While it is never easy when big things happen, you can learn to deal with it in the best possible way, mostly by letting others help you.

## KEEP COOL

## When it's time to talk

It's always good to talk through your problems with somebody else, but when really big things come up in families, it's even more important. Sometimes family stuff can be so overwhelming that it's best to talk with somebody outside your immediate family (you know, someone who's not so caught up in the drama). This might be an aunt or an uncle, a teacher you trust, a friend's parents or even a telephone helpline.

In addition to trusted others, sometimes it is necessary to talk to a professional counsellor or therapist who can help you learn to deal with whatever it is that is going on. They are often (but not always) available through your school or you can ask a trusted adult to sort one out for you.

There are great resources like ChildLine (see page 79) — who are set up to listen to you over the phone.

# Being able to cope

It's bad enough when something terrible happens, but it can seem even worse if you worry that you won't be able to cope with it. People get themselves into big trouble when they:

> OVER-estimate how bad the situation is (and is going to be)
> AND
> UNDER-estimate how able they are to cope with it.

For example, if your parents are getting divorced you might think, 'Gosh, this is a total disaster! My life will never be the same. I can't deal with this!'

This is your negative self-talk monster taking a bad situation and making it much worse. A better way to think of it would be more like, 'Gosh, this is really terrible and I feel just awful this has happened. I don't like it, but I'll survive and get as much support as I can.'

The situation is just as bad, but you are supporting yourself in it, instead of scaring yourself to death.

Most people actually can manage with the bad feelings that come up when terrible things happen (even though it still hurts). It's the FEAR that you won't be able to cope that makes a really bad situation feel much worse.

There are some really important things to remember when the heavy stuff happens:

**1.** You'll have lots and lots of different feelings including sadness, anger, fury, frustration, despair and more. All these feelings are natural. Don't fight them, talk about them.

**2.** You can cope with stuff far better than you believe that you can, you just need to take it one day at a time by not scaring yourself about the future.

**3.** It may not feel like it, but it actually does get better with time. You can speed that time along by talking.

*If you feel like you can't cope, it can be like the world is coming to an end. When you realise you can cope, you'll find it's not the end of the world after all.*

# Big family change

**When big family changes happen, it can feel like your entire world is falling apart.**

Lots of things can make you feel like this. Maybe an older brother or sister is moving out, or your parents are splitting up. Like other big stuff in life, there's no one thing you can do to make things better straight away. It's important to know that you can feel a thousand different ways about what's happening and that's okay: your feelings are yours.

## Divorce and separation

*What did I do wrong?*

If your parents are breaking up, you're going to have a lot of feelings about it. You may feel sad, but it's also common to feel angry or even relieved. While it's natural to feel pretty mixed-up, there are some feelings that aren't so helpful to you. For example, lots of kids blame themselves for their parents splitting up. They feel guilty because they feel they should have done something different to keep them together.

It's really important to know that parents split up because of problems between each other and not because of you. So don't torture yourself with those kinds of thoughts.

While a lot of decisions will have to be made about what happens if your parents split, if you're old enough to be reading this book, you're old enough to have some information about what's going on too. You should know about the stuff that involves you the most.

You might want to ask questions like:

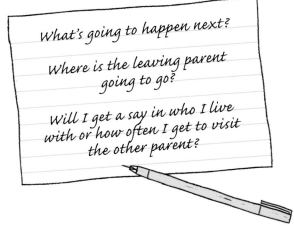

*What's going to happen next?*

*Where is the leaving parent going to go?*

*Will I get a say in who I live with or how often I get to visit the other parent?*

It's important that you sit and have a family meeting to answer as many of your questions as you can. The more you know, the more secure you will feel. Talking about how you are feeling about what's happening is, of course, really important too.

# What if someone dies?

One of the biggest things ANYONE has to deal with is the death of somebody that they love. It can be particularly hard when it happens in your family.

Sadly, somebody dying isn't something you can 'keep cool' about, it simply feels awful. More than any other time, when somebody dies you will need to lean on the people around you. You need to feel free to cry when you want to and even to scream if you have to. You will probably need lots of hugs too.

When somebody dies we go through a process called grieving which can make you feel all sorts of different ways. Lots of people get angry or hopeless, feel guilty or even laugh out loud without any reason! It helps to accept your feelings, whatever they are and talk them through with someone.

## When friends get weird about the big stuff*

We need our friends most when the really big stuff is happening. Unfortunately, these things can be so scary and so unthinkable that sometimes people just don't know what to do or say. Sometimes people that are very close to you mysteriously go silent: what's that about?

*What are we supposed to say?*

It's nothing you've done, it's just that those people don't know what to say – they just clam up!

Most of the time your friends will be okay again once they realise that you're still YOU no matter what happens. Sometimes your friends will need a little time to work that out. If you're having trouble with some friends clamming up because of what's happening in your life, try to talk to them about it. In the meantime, rely on those who CAN support you and when you feel ready, you can reach out to your other friends.

* You should read this section even if nothing 'big' is happening in your life. It can help you be a better friend to someone who is experiencing that. Try not to be one of those friends that 'clam up' — be one who your friends can lean on.

# Making it good

School takes up a major part of your life. Whether you like it or not, you've got to be there, so why not make the most of it? How do you see school? What colour glasses do you put on in the morning before going?

The way you think about school can really make a difference to your day. After all, school isn't JUST about learning, it's also about the teachers, your classmates, what happens in the playing fields, etc. In fact, school takes up so much of your head you probably think about it most of the time. How can you make it the best experience possible? Remember how your Bs (beliefs) will affect your Cs (consequences)? That works at school too.

## You've got attitude

Attitude is super important because it informs not just the way you feel inside, but also how you 'wear' those feelings in your body, and how that looks to others.

When your head is hanging low and your shoulders are hunched over, other people may respond to you more negatively. If you look like you don't expect much from others, they won't expect much from you - and that's a bad loop. A positive attitude does just the reverse! It's important to think about how your attitude affects the way you live in your body.

Take a look at Ivan. Can you see the difference between Ivan's positive and negative attitude through the way he holds his body?

Negative attitude Ivan

Positive attitude Ivan

### TRY IT OUT

## Body attitude

This is a really simple exercise that will surprise you. Stand in front of the mirror and imitate Negative Attitude Ivan's body posture. How does it look and feel? Next, try imitating Positive Attitude Ivan. Now how does that look and feel?

Isn't it amazing what a difference it makes just to change the way you stand there? Think about that before you leave in the morning for school.

# Fake it before you make it?

Walking into school confidently makes a huge difference, but that's hard if you're not FEELING it. In that case you might have to 'fake it before you make it'. That means trying to look confident even if you don't feel that way.

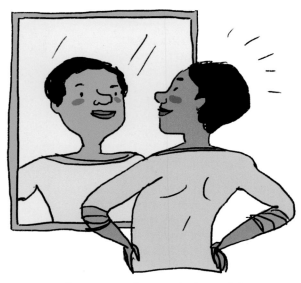

*When you make your body confident your feelings will shortly follow.*

Try it!* At first it will feel fake, like putting on a costume, but soon you'll start to believe it. It's like you have to teach your body how it feels to look confident and then the rest of you will catch on.

While it's not about wearing the right brands, trainers and stuff like that, a confident body deserves to look neat and tidy. When you leave home in the morning make sure there are no gobs of toothpaste on your face or food on your collar. Oh yeah and try not to smell bad by the end of the day either!

## KEEP COOL

## Starting at a new school

Starting at a new school CAN be pretty scary. Everything is new: the building, the rules, the teachers and new pupils too. What Bs (beliefs) will you bring with you to the new school? Will you be 'wearing' a positive attitude?

*Anxiety or excitement?*

Did you know that the feeling of anxiety is almost identical to the feeling of excitement? It's how you interpret the feeling that counts.** Everybody's nervous on the first day of school (even the teachers) so use that nervousness to your advantage: make it excitement instead!

Turn anxiety into excitement by reminding yourself that you can:

• meet new people and make new friends
• try new things and explore new areas
• take chances you were too scared to take before
• make a fresh start.

Don't leave it to chance. Burst through those doors on your first day with confidence and excitement.

* Be reasonable about it though. You don't want to be walking around like a peacock either!

** See, here come those perceptions again.

# Being at school

Being at school can be a challenge because you have to manage relationships with the teachers and other students, while worrying about taking part in class, your after school activities and just fitting in. What's the best way to meet the challenge of school?

## Taking risks

Why do people bungee jump? Because of the combination of fear and excitement that comes with the risk. If it weren't risky it wouldn't be half as exciting.

Sometimes things like these can make you feel like you're about to bungee jump:

- wondering if people will like you
- worrying people might laugh at you if you speak in front of the class
- being scared that you'll make a fool out of yourself in PE
- wondering if people will want you to sit next to them.

If fears like these hold you back from taking *some* risks, you'll never know what might happen or what opportunities you might miss. Don't scare yourself any more than you need to. Try not to confuse a smallish risk with a fear that's too big for it.

**KEEP COOL**

### Fear of Life or Death: *Really?*

Way back when humans lived in caves, we had to take our risks very seriously. If you offended your neighbour, they might come over and kill you. If you didn't hunt enough food to share with the village, the other villagers might run you out. If you weren't vigilant, you might be eaten by a sabre-toothed tiger!

We've evolved a lot since then, but our feelings haven't. Sometimes we feel like something is a life or death situation when it really isn't. We see an exam ahead as if it were a sabre-toothed tiger. We accidentally offend a friend and worry it's the end of our social life forever!

*Don't forget the test tomorrow!*

Next time you get 'the fear', check and see if you might be seeing sabre-toothed tigers where there aren't any.

# The risks of being social

Sometimes we can worry too much about being a social disaster. Does the fear of this sort of thing affect the decisions you make about the people you talk to or hang out with?

*Being forced into a box is not cool*

Schools can be intimidating because they are often full of groups and cliques. You've probably got names for certain groups at your school. You may be someone who identifies with one group, across a couple of groups, or you feel that you don't fit in any of them. You're not alone. Nobody fits SQUARELY into a single category. You're not JUST ONE THING, are you?

The trouble with school is that sometimes people think it's easier to put you in a box than to see you as a complex human being. The cool thing about school is that it's potentially a place where you can explore who you are in a whole lot of different ways.

What fears might be holding you back from taking some social risks at school? Is there some fear keeping you in a box? If you weren't in a box, who might you talk to, hang out with, eat lunch with? Wouldn't it be great if everyone came out of their boxes a little bit to see what else was around?

## KEEP COOL

## Invisible lines

There are lots of 'invisible lines' in the way we see each other at school. Like the way some people can hardly believe that the amazing athlete is also really good at maths; or the chess nerd is really good at hurdling. Can you think of the 'invisible lines' at your school? What feels like an invisible line you can't cross?

Don't let invisible lines hold you back from expressing yourself. Just because people think the shy kid wouldn't want to star in the school play doesn't make it true. What sorts of things do you think you can't do because of an invisible line? Is it time to think about them again?

*He can't cross THAT line!*

Some people think the 'cool' thing to do is to stay firmly behind that invisible line, but the real 'cool' people are the ones who won't be ruled by them.

# Study skills

Well done!

Worrying, stress and negative Bs (beliefs) are tightly connected to the way you study. If your head is full of worries, there will be a lot less room for more important stuff. By resolving your worries and stress, you can make studying a whole lot easier and (I'm not joking) more enjoyable.

By organising your time, and remembering how to use positive incentives well, you can really make studying a breeze. You can also help yourself (and your friends) by studying in groups on the same principles — just make sure you don't chat the whole time or work each other up into negative thinking!

## Homework

What was your thought when you saw the word 'homework'? Did you think 'ugh' — perhaps you will skip right over this page! Do you hate homework?

Well, let me ask you something: have you thought about what kind of glasses you wear when you think about homework? What was your perception here? What kind of Bs do you have about homework? While I won't convince you that homework is great fun, I can say that if you think it's really going to stink, it'll be even less fun than it needs to be.

HOME WORK

You can help yourself by doing your homework in the cool study space that you set up for yourself at home. That helps you make that positive association to do your work properly while you're there. As soon as you sit in your study space it's like a message to your brain that says, **'Time for work!'**

# Study time ...

First, choose a positive incentive to give yourself when it's all over. Something like planning to meet with a friend, going for a walk in the park or eating something nice. Make sure you are clear about what it is before you begin.

Once you're settled in to your work area, set a timer for your optimal work period.* Then turn off ALL your beeping devices: that means no windows open for Facebook, Twitter, email or anything else; put your phone on silent and stuff it under a pillow. Now, press go on your timer and get to work!

When your alarm goes, it's time for a short break. Make sure you get out of your chair and stretch and shake a little to get the blood moving again: it's important to do something mildly physical. Now you can check your phone, your Facebook etc. This whole process should take no more then ten minutes. Then set your clock and start work again.

Once you've finished for the day, help yourself to that positive incentive you put aside earlier. Enjoy that small reward for all the hard work you've accomplished. Well done!

* Your optimal work period is the time that works best for you. A lot of people find 45 minutes followed by a break works well. As a rough guide, don't study for less than 20 minutes and don't study any longer than an hour without a break. Try it out a few times to discover what works best for you.

# Exams

Guess what? Most of the worrying you do about exams isn't even about the exams. Think about it. When you worry, what are you REALLY worrying about? Look at Will.

Will has an exam at the end of the week and his first thought is 'If I fail this exam, my life will be over!'

Let's look at Will's thoughts more closely. Can you see some signs coming from his negative self-talk monster?

| 'If I fail this exam, my life will be over!' | |
| --- | --- |
| 1. What are the chances of Will actually FAILING the exam? | 2. Would Will's 'life be over'? Really? |
| A. How much evidence is there that he will fail? He could ask himself the questions on page 24.<br>B. If there is evidence that he could fail, what can he learn from that?<br>What can he do to respond positively to it?<br>C. Is Will overestimating how difficult the exam will be while underestimating his ability to cope with it? | A. What does he mean by this? It would be a disappointment, but would his life really be over?<br>B. If the worst happened and Will did fail, would it really be a total disaster? Could he re-sit? What are his options? |

When Will really thinks it through properly, it's not nearly so scary. How much time do you spend worrying about imagined catastrophes at the expense of just knuckling down to your studying?

## Is it really a catastrophe?

**Catastrophising** is a thing that you do when you look ahead to some event in the future and think if BLANK happens, it will be a CATASTROPHE! It's also called **awfulising**. That's like, 'If it doesn't go exactly my way, it will be AWFUL!'

There's a big difference between looking at what might happen if it doesn't go your way and planning for that, and creating disaster scenarios. Can you see how Will is catastrophising? Have you ever caught yourself doing that?

If you find yourself catastrophising, ask yourself two simple questions:

> **1.** What are the chances (really) that the thing you're worried about will actually happen?
>
> **2.** If it DID happen, would it really be a total catastrophe?

This only works if you answer the questions honestly. It might help to do that in your journal. Of course, sometimes things don't go your way, but that hardly makes them a catastrophe. By taking the fear of the catastrophe out of the picture, you can get down to the business of keeping your cool.

# Visualise it going well!

Instead of catastrophising, why don't you try **positive visualisation**?

The night before your exam, just close your eyes, take a deep breath and imagine yourself walking into your exam feeling cool and confident. Imagine yourself sitting down, opening the exam and then KICKING BUTT! Go through the whole process. Then imagine putting the exam down, standing up and walking out confidently.

This is like a practice run for your brain — when you arrive the next morning, it will be as if your brain has already done it, and you'll be amazed at how confident you feel.

**TRY IT OUT**

# Breathe! Don't panic

Whenever you feel like you're going to panic about something, there is a very simple way to calm down. Just breathe!

It sounds silly because of course we all breathe anyway, but when we get really nervous and start to panic our breathing gets faster and more shallow. This means less oxygen gets to your brain, you start to feel woozy and you panic more.

So next time you panic:

1. Notice you're panicking, then tell yourself gently to 'slow down'.
2. Take a really deep breath through your nose and exhale slowly through your mouth (it might help to count to five during each breath).
3. Do this five to ten times, slowing everything down along the way.
4. All the while, feel your feet on the ground as you breathe – this will help to bring you down to earth.

# After school activities

Every weekday shouldn't be ALL ABOUT SCHOOL. After all, you are more than just a student, and you should develop other parts of your life too. It's really important to develop your personality in a whole range of different directions.*

Remember when we talked about filling up your jar with coins? First you practised that as a way to understand your self-image, and then how to help your family work better. It turns out that your one big jar is actually made up of lots of smaller ones, each with a different label.

How would you label your jars?
Are some emptier than others?
Which ones do you think need filling up?

## When it's not so cool at school

KEEP COOL

If you're unhappy at school you might think you'll be unhappy doing stuff outside school too. When that happens, you've got a bad loop, and it's time to take a bad loop and make it into a good one by changing your Bs.

Whether it's scouts or brownies, local theatre, sports, art groups, singing groups or whatever, these are opportunities to expand your personality, improve your attitude, and put coins in your jar.

*Don't let negative thinking get in the way of a great opportunity.*

When school is an unhappy place, activities outside of school can give you a chance to meet new people and for you to choose a way to express yourself differently. If you feel positive about the stuff you do outside of school, that attitude is likely to filter into how you feel about life in general — including school!

* Remember your personality inventory on page 11? After school activities can help you meet more parts of your personality than just school alone.

Now think back to all the work you've been doing about your personality, your beliefs, and your self-image. Now think about risk. Are you prepared to change your Bs a little to take a risk you normally wouldn't?

Have a look at the spider diagram you did on page 13. What sorts of activities can you think of that might help you put coins in the jars of those areas in your life?

By looking outside school you can actually improve your self-image (fill up that jar with coins) and you are able to come back to school feeling better about yourself and more secure.

By increasing your activities (not decreasing them) you give yourself a chance to make things better at school too! So keep an open mind and try it out.

Have a look at the spider diagram you did on page 13.

**TRY IT OUT**

## Finding YOUR after school activity

If you haven't found a cool thing to do outside of school, get to work now and find something! It probably won't come to you, so you have to go to it.

Prop yourself in front of a computer for an hour and search out things that are interesting to you and that are in your local area. Compile some research (what's the thing, who to contact, what's their number, what days do they meet, will it fit your schedule, how much does it cost etc.) and make a shortlist. Take the list to your parents and make some phone calls.

CHESS

POTTERY    THEATRE

BALLROOM DANCING

VIOLIN

PHOTOGRAPHY

BASKETBALL

**Don't wait for it to happen, make it happen!**

## Good friends

There are times in your life when your friends become at least as important to you as your family. What your friends think of you can seem like the most important thing in the world, but what you think of yourself is even more important.

Real quality friends show respect and support and should help you feel better about yourself, not worse. In addition to being able to have a good laugh with them, good friends:

- can be trusted and relied upon
- don't expect you to be anybody but yourself
- will listen to you when you talk and won't be judgmental
- can keep your secrets and confidences
- will care about what happens to you.

Really close friendships can take some time to develop. Remember it's always a matter of quality, not quantity. One good trusted friend beats a dozen folks you hang out with but can't trust.

If you hang out with some people who continually make you feel bad, leave you out of things and in general make life unpleasant, is it really worth trying to keep things going with them?

## New friends: The hardest thing is saying 'hello'

All of us have different levels of shyness and it's okay to feel shy. However, if your shyness is getting in the way of making friends, it's important to deal with it if you can.

It feels risky to take that first step, but if your fear of that risk holds you back you could miss the opportunity to hang out with some people you might really like. The riskiest part of making a new friend is that first step: just saying 'hello'.

The good news is that it gets easier after that. If you can get your courage together to walk over to someone and say 'hello' the worst is already over in two seconds! You've broken the ice and now you're free to talk about all sorts of things. If the conversation dries up, just ask a question about the other person. People love to talk about themselves!

# When there's trouble, talk it through

Most of the time we get on pretty well with our friends, but of course sometimes things can go wrong. Conflict comes along at some point in every friendship. Staying friends isn't as much about totally avoiding conflict as it is being able to respond to it well. Just like with families, trust and communication are the keys to resolving problems.

If you've got a beef with a friend, don't sit on it, talk about it. Holding grudges and expecting your friend to work out why you're mad is NOT the best way to move forward. One of the biggest mistakes you can make with a friend is thinking you can mind read them and that they should be able to mind read you.

*I want to talk to her, but she doesn't want to talk to me!*

*I want to talk to her, but she doesn't want to talk to me!*

## Mind reading

Mind reading is when you think you know what somebody else is thinking and then make decisions based on that. When you're both mind reading (and you usually are) it can be a disaster waiting to happen because both of you are operating on assumptions rather than real information.

*Can we talk?*

*I'm so relieved, I was so hoping she'd say that.*

## Mind reading doesn't give you the facts, only talking does.

You might be scared to start a conversation because there are so many bad feelings around. If you use what you learned about the timing of important conversations, active listening and using 'I' language (see pages 28 and 29) you'll find talking about it much easier.

Now, don't you think it's time to stop trying to read minds and get talking the truth instead?

# Bullying
## What actually is bullying?

Bullying is repeated and aggressive behaviour (physical, verbal or emotional) that is intended to hurt another person. It is never okay, and it is not just 'ribbing' or 'taking the piss'.

Nobody likes it, but unfortunately bullying happens, especially at school. While the next few pages will tell you how to deal with bullies better, you shouldn't face down bullies on your own. All schools in the UK have a bullying policy — so if you are being bullied, make sure you find out about it and put it to use.

The single best thing you can do to combat bullying is to talk about it. Don't keep it to yourself. The bully actually gains power by keeping you quiet. Keep your cool by finding the person you trust most and telling them. They can help make sure your school helps you sort it out.

**KEEP COOL**

## Does bullying start at home?

It's a sad but true fact that brothers and sisters often bully each other, and parents and step-parents* can bully their children too.

About a third of kids are bullied by their siblings, and lots of these kids will go on to be bullied at school too. Often parents don't know this is going on because they think it's 'just the kids fighting'. If it's relentless and you have become scared of your brother or sister, it's not just 'kids fighting' anymore.

If this is happening to you at home, make sure you tell someone. Solving a bullying problem at home will do wonders for your problems at school too.

---

* It's terrible when it happens, but some parents do bully their children. This can be really serious and if it's happening to you, you need to tell someone you trust. If you're feeling scared, a good first stop is to call ChildLine (see page 79) who can help you come to your own solution to the problem.

# Preventing it in the first place

However scary bullies are, they actually are pretty wimpy because they only pick fights they think they can win. That's why they often bully in groups, and pick on people who they think will let them get away with it.

You can reduce your chances of being bullied by following the advice on confidence and attitude on pages 42 and 43. By holding your head up high, presenting a strong and positive attitude to the world you make it less likely that they will come after you. Being confident and topping up your self-image is like covering yourself with anti-bullying spray.

Bullies try to lower your self-image by stealing the coins out of your jar. They may threaten you or talk to you in ways that make you feel bad about yourself. Don't let them get in your head. Guard your coins with your life. They are not for somebody else to take.

**KEEP COOL**

## Why bullies bully

Why do bullies bully?
Some reasons might be because:

- they have been bullied themselves
- they are having problems at home
- they feel insecure and take that out on you (by stealing your coins they feel they are getting them for themselves)
- they want to look 'important' in front of their friends
- they haven't quite worked out how much it hurts or even that they are a bully
- they haven't realised that they are being a bully.

Each bully is different but they generally bully because they need to sort themselves out, not because you are doing something wrong.

If YOU are a bully it's a brave thing to accept about yourself. Once you realise how the person you bully feels, you'll want to stop. That can be hard if you don't know other ways to deal with your feelings so talk to someone who can help.

# Responding to what bullies DO

Finding a solution to a bullying problem can be tricky, so don't try to do it on your own. Work with somebody else to find the best solution for your situation.*

The best response to a bully is a disarming one (one they don't expect from you):

— You can say NO to them firmly and leave.

— You can act like you don't care, refuse to listen to them or respond to them and just walk away.

— You can respond with something unexpected and funny (maybe something you thought up beforehand).

- If they come after you physically, avoid a fight if at all possible. Get away from the problem first and call for help, especially if it's a gang. Defending yourself physically should be a last resort.

— If you are forced to defend yourself, do it: then get away and call for help.

— You can build up your self-esteem by taking martial arts or self-defence classes. You may never need to use it, but it will make you feel more confident and secure.

- Don't let bullies get the satisfaction of seeing that they've got under your skin. When confronted, try to hold it together by not taking the bait, not looking afraid (even if you are) and doing your best not to cry in front of them.**

- Keep a record of all the times you get bullied and what happened to help the school deal with it properly.

* Use the tactics that best suit your personality; different things work for different people.

** Of course it's fine to cry once you've got away, but it's best not to give them the satisfaction of knowing they've got to you.

# Responding to how bullies make you feel

The worst thing about bullies isn't really what they DO to you, it's how they can make you feel about yourself. A bully can get into your head and affect your negative self-talk. As you know, that can decrease your self-esteem and make you feel fearful and helpless all the time.

When that happens it's like you've got a bully in your head. The bully in your head is especially bad because there's no safe place away from it. The bully in your head can get you at home, even when you're safe in bed.

Is there a bully in your head?
Are they dressed up like your negative self-talk monster making you have more negative Bs? Time to go back to those monster killing exercises (like looking at your jars and checking the evidence).

While it takes time, the single best thing you can do is to build your confidence. You do that by finding all the ways you can to:

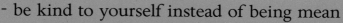

- be kind to yourself instead of being mean
- do everything you can (with the help of others) to build up your self-confidence.

Filling your jar should now become a mission. Look at the section on after school activities (page 51) and get into one that you really enjoy. Make sure you do something physical too. This is not to get stronger than bullies, but to help you feel more strong and secure in your own body. You might think about trying something like martial arts (judo or taekwondo): you probably won't beat anybody up, but you'll learn to defend yourself better, and you'll probably enjoy it too.

# Cyberbullying

As if it weren't difficult enough to keep the bullies out of school and out of your head, now you have to keep them off your phone, your social networking, your email, your chat and loads of other places too.

Prevention is by far the most important thing for cyberbullying.
Make it as difficult as possible for people to get at you in cyberspace.
It's common sense, but it's worth doing the following:

- Understand your digital technology.
  – Learn about the settings of all the technology you use and make sure you have control over them.
  – Keep passwords safe and don't share them with anyone but your parents.

- Keep information like phone numbers, addresses and email addresses private. Only give them to people you know and trust.
  – Know what other information about you to keep to yourself.

- Only have people you know on your social networks.
  – If you want to make new friends, make sure they are at least known (I mean in real life) to one of your other friends.

- Be aware that ANYTHING you send (text, photos, information) can be replicated and distributed with the click of a button.

- If something dodgy is happening, like you're getting nasty messages from an unknown source, tell an adult.

If you're being cyberbullied, there are three main things to consider:

1. Talking to an adult about it.

2. Working out how you handle the situation in cyberworld with your internet service provider, mobile phone operator or whatever platform you're being bullied on.

3. How to handle your own reactions within yourself to what is going on.

First, identify where (on what platform) something happened. If you are being harassed on Facebook then contact the Facebook team to get it sorted. Similarly, if someone has put up a nasty video on YouTube, created a nasty website or is sending you nasty text messages, inform YouTube, the website provider, or your mobile telephone network.

HELLO SPOTTY, I HATE YOU...

**website provider**

THE INTERNET

Even though it's pretty awful to look at, the stuff in cyberworld is evidence against your bully, so take screenshots of the nasty stuff, save abusive emails in a file and don't delete the nasty texts: you can use these against the bullies. But remember that you are keeping this as evidence. It can be upsetting, so avoid looking at it more than necessary. Save it, put it away, and then use it when you need to.

It's important to know that harassment is actually illegal. That means if you are being harassed online (or anywhere else) you can call the police. By saving all the evidence, you can help the police deal with it better.

DO get the support of your family to do these things. DON'T do it alone.

At some stage you might need to start over either with a new profile, a new phone number or a new email address. With a new clean slate, make sure you use the prevention tips on the previous page to prevent it from happening again.

# More than friends

As if regular friendships weren't complicated enough, managing romantic relationships can be really confusing. The good news is that most of the time you are both confused together, so you're in the same boat!

## How do I know he/she is into me?

Flirting is a skill, and it can take some time to get it right. Flirting is all about sending signals to each other and working out if you both want to take your relationship to the next level. The signs can be pretty subtle (though sometimes not so much!) so keep your eyes and ears open.

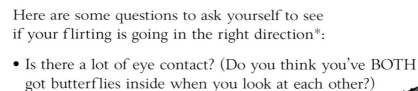

Here are some questions to ask yourself to see if your flirting is going in the right direction*:

- Is there a lot of eye contact? (Do you think you've BOTH got butterflies inside when you look at each other?)
- Are they laughing at your jokes (even if they're not funny)?
- Is the body language about getting closer or further apart?
- Is the person making excuses to hang out with you longer or trying to get away?
- Is the conversation flowing or full of awkward silences?

## When friendship turns romantic

It's pretty common that good friends sometimes fall for each other. While good relationships often start out as good friendships, it can still be pretty scary to make a move. That's because sometimes you get those uncomfortable situations where one friend falls for the other, but the other one just wants to be friends (I know, CRINGE).

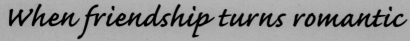

* You'll notice that you can't find out any of these things with online flirting. While flirting online is fine, you'll never get the kind of information you really need to move on, so try not to keep your flirting exclusive to messages across a network.

If you're the one who fancies a friend, it's time to be alert to all those signs we've just talked about to see if they are feeling the same way. If things are going in your direction, then it might be time to let your friend know you want to move things on. If not, it's up to you to re-double your flirting, have a serious conversation with them or gently back down.

If things work out, brilliant! You're sorted! But if they don't, chances are you won't lose your good friend forever. Really good friends will 'get it'. Sure, it will feel uncomfortable for a while, but you'll both find your way back again soon enough.

If you happen to be the object of your friend's affections but you don't feel the same way, be sensitive and respectful to

the friend that has a crush on you. Tell them gently that you'd prefer to keep things as they are. It's something you should feel flattered about, not weird or ashamed: so try to let them down gently.

## But what if I get rejected?

If there's one thing that scares the pants off people it's rejection. They think, 'If I ask them and they say no, it will be a disaster!' I'm not going to lie to you and say it doesn't hurt (in fact it does, pretty much every time). Still, fear of rejection

also prevents lots of people from taking a chance to see if someone might say 'yes'.

Everybody's scared of rejection. It's just one of those fears we have to learn to live with because if we are guided by that fear, we end up rejecting ourselves before anybody else has the chance!

Asking someone out is a bit like making a bet — you just want the odds to be in your favour. Taking the advice in this chapter will help you hedge your bets, but there's no 'sure thing'. Whatever happens, there's more of a chance of them saying yes if you ask than if you don't!

## There's no rush

Getting a girlfriend or boyfriend can be great, but only when you're ready. Don't rush into it or feel like it's something you have to do.

# Sexuality and gender is for everyone

Sexuality and gender are two really important things that make up who you are and how you feel about yourself.

**Sexuality** has to do with the kind of person you fancy or fall in love with, who you want to cuddle, kiss and fool around with.

**Gender** is about whether you feel more girly (feminine) or boyish (masculine) whatever sex your body is.

There are lots of expectations about what it means to be a boy or a girl: but there's no right or wrong way to be either one.

The world is full of stereotypes that tell us how we 'should be'. Just like people aren't in boxes (see page 45), people don't fit neatly into stereotypes either.

## Here are some stereotypes about gender:

- Girls are feminine. They like pink, don't like sports, and love shopping.

- Boys are masculine. They like blue, are into sport and are really tough.

- Girls should stick with girl stuff and boys should stick with boy stuff.

While some of these things are true about *some* boys and girls, they are not true about all of them. There are loads of way to be!

Some boys aren't crazy about typical 'boy things' and some girls just can't stand 'girly things'.

*I hate sport!*

*I hate pink!*

When it comes to sexuality, you can't make assumptions about people either. After all, while lots of girls and boys fancy each other, some girls fancy other girls, some boys fancy other boys, and some folks don't mind

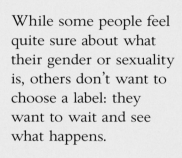

While some people feel quite sure about what their gender or sexuality is, others don't want to choose a label: they want to wait and see what happens.

what the gender of the other person that they fancy is. Other people don't feel particularly sexual about anyone.

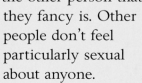

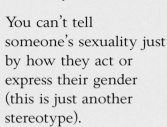

You can't tell someone's sexuality just by how they act or express their gender (this is just another stereotype).

While there's absolutely no rush to label yourself as anything, some people like to so they can find other folks who feel like they do. Some might choose from the following labels:

Lesbian: girls who fancy girls

Gay: boys who fancy boys (you can also say 'gay girl' or 'gay woman')

Straight: boys who fancy girls and girls who fancy boys

Queer: someone who feels their sexuality is 'fluid' and doesn't want to be tied down (this applies to gender too)

Bisexual or Bi: someone who fancies both boys and girls

Asexual or A: someone who doesn't really feel sexual attraction to others

# Transgender

Some people may be 'transgendered' or just 'trans'. This has different meanings for different people, but usually trans people feel that the sex they were told they were when they were born (male or female) doesn't neatly match how they feel in themselves. For example, someone with a boy's body may feel more like a girl, or someone born with a girl's body may feel

more like a boy. Sometimes they may feel in between being a boy or a girl, or different to either of these. It's important to note that transgender is not about sexuality. A trans-person could be straight, gay, bi, queer or asexual.

Note: Biologically not all people are born as either a boy or a girl. Some folks have aspects of both, and are called intersex.

# Some folks don't like what they can't understand

Depending on your family, your culture or religion, and where you live, it will be harder or easier to express those genders and sexualities that fall outside stereotypes. Sadly, many people feel that they have to keep their sexuality quiet for fear that they will be bullied about it or even kicked out of their homes.

GET OUT!

I don't know!

While it's not necessary to choose a label or make any announcements until you're good and ready, it is important that you give it good thought and not feel ashamed of who you are. Get support about your feelings if you can. Talk it over with someone you can trust. If you can't find that person, there are some resources on page 79 that can help you make a start.

We are what we are and we're proud of it!

If you don't fit into a stereotype, people can make life hard on you; it's not fair, but unfortunately it happens. It's important not to let people like that get into your head and make you feel ashamed of who you are. If you run into trouble with these sorts, check out the section on bullying and get some support. Your gender and sexuality is YOURS - don't let people try to stuff you into boxes that don't fit.

## It gets better

It can be a confusing time if you come to realise that your gender or your sexuality is different from most other people you know. It helps to know that after what might be a confusing time, it does get better. Check out the links on page 79 to hear stories about people's journeys about their gender and sexuality.

If you know someone who is struggling with their sexuality or gender, reach out a hand to them. Be a good friend, listen and be supportive.

## Coming out

You are in a part of your life where you'll be experiencing lots of changes and different sorts of feelings. There's no need to make any major decisions about who or what you are. Maybe you've fooled around with a guy or a girl, and you think that might mean you're gay or lesbian. It doesn't. You don't have to put a label on anything unless you want to. And you don't have to tell anyone until you're good and ready.

Some folks are pretty sure. If this is the case there may come a time when you wish to tell your family and friends. Thinking about these points will help:

1 Tell the safest person you know first. Make sure they'll support you if you want to announce it to others.
2 Make sure you choose the right time and place to tell family (see page 29 on timing).
3 Remember that you've known this for some time, and it may be a surprise to your family, so give them time to get used to it. They might ask some questions.
4 Make sure there's a safe person to talk to if it doesn't go well with your family.
5 Be smart about who you tell. News travels fast, so make sure you're good and ready.
6 Feel proud of yourself. It's a brave thing to do.

# Feeling frisky*

Of all the weird and crazy worries people have, the ones about sex really take the biscuit. That's because many people find it hard to talk about sex and there are an awful lot of myths flying around about it.

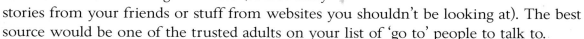

*THAT WAS ROMANTIC!*

Just like anything, the more you know about sex, the less mystery there is about it and the less you need to worry. The first step in keeping cool about sexual matters is to get the right information from the right sources (so not crazy stories from your friends or stuff from websites you shouldn't be looking at). The best source would be one of the trusted adults on your list of 'go to' people to talk to.

Most importantly, sexual feelings are nothing to be ashamed of. We all have them, and when you are going through puberty you can have them pretty strongly. Around puberty you will probably be very curious about changes going on in your body. It also means that you're likely to have erotic dreams and daydreams, you may also be masturbating or experimenting with other people.

All of this is totally natural and nothing to be afraid of. You just want to make sure you're making the best possible decisions for yourself as you go along. Whenever you try something new there's always a bit of bumbling around, and being sexual is no different, so try not to let it worry you any more than anything else.

## How do I know when I'm ready?

Everybody becomes ready to be sexual** at a different time.
There are good and bad reasons to be sexual. Some good reasons are:

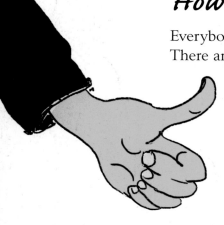

- because you feel ready and you both want to
- because you love and trust the person you are with
- because you've thought it through and talked it over
- because you know you can say 'no' when you want to
- because you've considered all the consequences and know about safety (see Further resources on page 79).

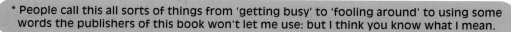

* People call this all sorts of things from 'getting busy' to 'fooling around' to using some words the publishers of this book won't let me use: but I think you know what I mean.

**When I say 'sexual' here I mean it in the broadest sense from snogging to going all the way.

Some bad reasons are:

- because other people are doing it
- because you feel pressured to do it
- because you think you'll be rejected if you don't
- because you can't say 'no'.

# It takes two to tango

Being sexual with each other is best when there is mutual trust and respect. As soon as one person gets uncomfortable or feels pressured, it becomes a whole lot less fun for everyone and scary for the person under pressure. It's important to make sure both partners are okay.

While it's hard enough to talk about sex anyway, it's actually super important that you can talk about it with the person you're fooling around with. You need to be able to say, 'Let's stop there' or, 'That makes me uncomfortable.'

It's also important to ask, 'Is this okay?' or 'Are you comfortable with what's happening?'

The more trust and communication you have, the better the experience will be. Whatever happens, don't even START to mess around with someone unless you have all the information you need to move forward (see resources on page 79). It's important that you trust them and that you trust yourself to know you'll say 'no' if and when you want to.

# What's consent?

Consent is another word for permission. Being sexual in any way without consent is not only harmful and disrespectful, but it's against the law. If someone says 'no' then they are not giving consent, no matter what happened before that.

In the UK the age of consent for sex is 16. This means that it's not legal to have sex if you are under 16. If you are older and have sex with someone under 16 then you are breaking the law. Even though different people become sexual at different ages, this law is intended to protect as many people as possible.

# Being you and being you with them

We hear the phrase 'be yourself' all the time, but that can be hard when we are surrounded by people who may want us to be someone we are not. Lots of people have different expectations of us and that can be confusing. Just think, what does your father, your mother, your teacher, your best friend or your dog want from you?

It can be pretty tough to respond to the needs of those close to us, while also being ourselves. While it's important to keep in mind what others need of us, you should also be aware of what you need to be happy.

## KEEP COOL

## Being assertive

Some people think that life is either about being demanding and getting what you want, or letting people walk all over you. It doesn't have to be either. That's what being assertive is about. When you are **assertive**, you stand up for who you are and what you need, while still being respectful of others.

Being assertive goes hand in hand with being sure of yourself. It will help you in life with friends, relationships, and facing up to bullies.

A big part of being assertive is the art of saying 'NO' when you need to. When you know something isn't right for you, even if there is pressure, you need to know that you can say 'No thanks,' and if that doesn't work, a short simple, 'I said NO.'

By practising the exercises throughout this book, you can build confidence that helps with assertion. Remember, assertion isn't being stubborn, it's being clear about what you need/want.

# Peer pressure

When you're with a group of people who want you to do something you don't want to do, being assertive can be tough.

Especially with pressure around:

- smoking, drinking and the food you eat
- how people think your body should look
- whether or not you try drugs
- who to like and who not to like (and who to hang out with and who not to)
- how you should dress, act, etc.
- how much you should study, do sports or other activities
- what music, games, television programmes you should like or not.

It's actually pretty incredible how much power people and groups can have to make us conform. But if we let that happen, we'd all be the same.

You probably worry about doing things right to 'fit in' — you might look to the popular kids or the leaders of whatever clique or group you're in to see what the right thing to do is. You might even be a leader of a group and still feel pressure to do something you don't want to do.

While it's fine to be part of a group, it's not fine when that group tries to make you do something you don't want to do. When that happens, it's time to stand up for yourself confidently and assertively.

**TRY IT OUT**

## A total expression of you

Imagine if there were NO limits. I mean NO ONE to tell you how you should look or how you should behave. What would that be like? In the real world, there are always limits, but not necessarily in your mind.

On a separate piece of paper, draw your fantasy you: the kind of clothes you'd wear, how you'd do your hair, the kind of things you'd be doing. Go crazy! While you may not want to go around looking like that in the real world, it can give you an insight into how you might want to express yourself.

# Being connected

Modern life can seem like it's ALL about being connected up to technology. Underneath, though, it's really all about relationships, isn't it? I mean, after all what are you DOING all the time on Twitter, Facebook or texting if you're not chatting, commenting or texting with somebody else? Even if you're a gamer, you're probably playing games with other people from all around the world.

The trick with technology is to make sure you don't value it over the relationship.

Letting tech rule your life isn't a recipe for calm, is it? While we all think we can multi-task, we actually do stuff better one thing at a time. Focusing on one thing at a time makes you feel calmer too.

We already talked about managing tech in relation to getting homework done and studying for exams, but how does it affect the rest of your life? Think particularly about the relationships in your life — does tech get in the way?

## KEEP COOL

## Technetiquette (or good manners with technology)

*This call can wait. I'm listening to you right now.*

How would you feel if you were talking to somebody and they just suddenly stopped listening and turned their head towards someone else and started talking to them? Not so cool, huh?

This is exactly what you are doing when you pick up your phone to check a text while talking to your friend or someone in your family.

The first rule of techniquette is that real people come first. Make this clear with your family and friends. When you're with each other, take the time to actually BE with each other and not your technology. It can be hard, but it definitely helps build stronger relationships and decreases stress.

# Tech-free

If family and friends aren't good at their 'techniquette' you can feel like they aren't paying proper attention or listening to you. It's the same way around if you're obsessed with tech and not listening to them.*

By having some tech-free zones (like in the car with your family or at the dinner table) you'll find that there's a lot more time to spend with each other and not just our machines. It might seem hard or weird, but try it out and see where you get.

TRY IT OUT

## Grounding yoga

Sometimes you can get so caught up in technology that your head is in the clouds. Using your own body to come back down to Earth is a great antidote to too much technology. Yoga can help centre and ground you. So, take a break from tech, get into your Zen space and try some grounding yoga.

**1** Take your shoes off and just stand up, paying special attention to your feet on the floor. Notice how the solid ground feels to your feet, all the way up your legs and into your knees, up your spine and all the way to your head.

**2** Stand for a moment breathing deeply and just appreciate the solid ground under your feet.

**3** Then, bit by bit, starting with your knees, slowly relax the rest of your body onto the floor. Notice how each part of your body feels as it touches the ground.

**4** When your whole body is on the floor, notice how it feels, especially the parts in contact with the hard floor.

**5** Rest there for some time breathing deeply and connecting to the ground.

**6** If you can, when it's warm and dry, try this outside on the grass or if you get the chance, on a sandy beach. Then you really feel the Earth beneath your feet.

* This can be especially true of parents who sometimes need reminding to put their mobiles down to give you their undivided attention.

# The Social Network

Social networking is like the air we breathe when it comes to communicating with our friends. It lets you keep in touch 24/7 with your mates, share all sorts of stuff about your life with groups of friends, even with those who have moved far away. It literally keeps you connected.

*What on EARTH are you doing there dear?*

It's important to be mindful about what you share and who you share it with. Once stuff is online, it's very easy for it to spread and multiply everywhere — it's much easier to put something up than to take it down. As a rule of thumb, don't put stuff up that you wouldn't want your gran to see — and be aware that even stuff you send privately can be at risk.*

**KEEP COOL**

## Am I addicted to tech?

'Addicted' is a pretty serious word, but it's important to work out if you are spending too much time online and if you are, to take some steps to reduce it. You can tell if you're spending too much time online by honestly answering the following questions:

1. Do you lose sleep because you are online (or gaming) into the small hours?
2. When you're not online, are you thinking about going online?
3. Do you get anxious when you can't go online for a while?
4. Are you struggling in school, sport or other activities because of the time you spend online?
5. Does time on the Internet get in the way of time with friends and family?
6. Do you often stay online longer than you mean to?
7. Have you ever lied about how much you've been online?

If you answered 'yes' to a lot of these questions, it may be time to reconsider your Internet/gadget use and get some support to reduce it. Even if you only said 'yes' to one or two, keep aware of your usage and try introducing more breaks.

* See page 58 for info on how to keep control of your online information.

# Online rules to live by

There are certain 'rules' you just know about when it comes to your friends. Things like not embarrassing them in front of their other friends, not being mean to them, not being nasty about them behind their backs and not telling their secrets to everyone you know*.

There are similar rules for social networking but they're easier to forget when you're sitting in front of a computer on your own. In some ways the consequences are worse because your mistake is up there for everyone to see!

## DO: ✔

- be respectful
- know that potentially anybody can see what you post
- take stuff down when somebody asks you to
- be yourself, but be aware of your privacy and your cybershadow.

## DON'T: ✘

- put up embarrassing photos of your friends (when in doubt, ask them first)
- put stuff up that will intentionally make someone else feel left out, embarrassed or hurt
- put up information about other people that they wouldn't want to share
- cut and paste private messages and make them public
- participate in cyberbullying.

Think about getting together with your friends and making an agreement about your own dos and don'ts.

**KEEP COOL**

## Your cybershadow

Everything you put online could be there forever. Even if you take it down, someone may have already taken a screenshot or a little spider on Google may have picked it up. It's important to be aware that even if you don't care about it right now, you might in a few years (you want your future employer to see THAT photo of you?). Have fun, but be careful and keep aware.

*YOUR CYBERSHADOW WILL FOLLOW YOU WHEREVER YOU GO.*

* Yes, we all slip up sometimes, but in general you try to keep these sorts of rules, right?

# Your future

When you go out to run an assault course you know what to expect. It's not like you run 100 metres and stop and ask, 'Hey, what are these tyres doing here?' Of course you don't because the tyres are part of the course!

The tyres aren't there to get in your way; they are part of the fun. Life is a bit like an assault course. The trouble with some people is that when something happens in their life that they don't expect to see they say, 'Hey, what's that doing in my way?' Wouldn't it be better if they just saw that thing, just like you see the tyres in an assault course?

As you start to achieve your goals for the future, it's important to realise that there will be tyres along the way (and walls to climb, and tubes to crawl through, and slimy water to wade through too!). Those challenges aren't getting in your way, they are part of that assault course we call life. Make sure your Bs see them as challenges rather than obstacles.

## KEEP COOL  Fail your way to success?

'Failure' is a bad word. It literally means 'unsuccessful' — so how can somebody fail his or her way to success? If you think of any person you admire, such as an athlete, an actor or entrepreneur, the chances are that they failed a bit before becoming successful. The path to success isn't about avoiding failure, it's about accepting it as part of life and moving on.

*If at first you don't succeed...*

If you want to be a skier and you never fall down, you're probably not challenging yourself enough and you'll never get to the Olympics. If you ski and you occasionally fall, you know you're working at the edge of your capability and getting better all the time.

So while you shouldn't try to fail, you should know that failure isn't such a bad thing. Thinking that failure is 'the end' is just catastrophising, and we know that's no good. How might you see failure as an opportunity?

# Achieving your goals

Do you know what your goals are? Maybe you have some vague ideas, such as going to university, becoming a top chef or breaking a sporting record. The clearer your idea of what you want, the more chance you have of achieving it. In order to achieve your goals, it helps to break them down by asking the following questions:

*What is my goal?*

*When can I achieve my goal?*

*Working backwards, what steps can I do to achieve my goal?*

*What can I do today?*

The best motivation to achieve a goal is if it's yours. If you're trying to do it for someone else, you'll never work as hard — so think it through carefully.

Work backwards. Think of the date when you (realistically) want it to be achieved. WRITE THAT DATE DOWN — put it in your calendar.

If your goal is in a year's time, where do you need to be in six months? Two months? Next week?

Try to take one action each day, however small, to achieve your goal and you'll know you're moving forward.

---

**TRY IT OUT**

## Goal collage

It's best to use all your resources to motivate you to achieve your goals. Making a collage is a great way to MAKE it and SEE it.

You'll need:
A massive piece of card, a load of old magazines, scissors and some glue

Now attack those magazines and cut out all the pictures you can that represent your goal. Use actual photos, images, words and symbols too. Paste them artistically on your card with the most important symbol of your goal right in the middle. You can add to it over time, and put it some place special in 'your space' that you created earlier.

# NOW THAT YOU'RE COOL

You were pretty cool to start with, but now you should have a few pockets-full of great practical advice and information about how to stay chilled out, less stressed and cool as a cucumber.

Now I don't know a single person who is cool all the time, so there's no reason why you should be. The best you can do is to practise the exercises in this book and learn to deal with worries and stresses a little bit better all the time.

If you put the skills you learn here into regular practice, they can help you for the rest of your life.

Always remember though, that you can't handle everything on your own and we all need each other to get on. So when you see someone you know who's stressed and worried, the best thing to do is to listen to them first. Then you can teach them everything you know about keeping cool, so they become cool too. After all, there's enough cool to go around...

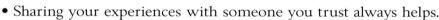

## Keep cool checklist

Here's a quick and handy guide of things to remember to make sure you're keeping cool.

- Sharing your experiences with someone you trust always helps.
- You may not be able to change the stuff that happens to you, but you can change your perceptions and beliefs about those things.
- Writing a journal helps you to process and externalise all your thoughts and feelings.
- Keep an eye on all aspects of your life including the physical, mental, emotional, social and spiritual.
- Your self-image can be improved by putting coins in your jar. You can do that by being aware of your accomplishments and making them count.
- You're aware that you can sometimes be nasty to yourself and you know how to beat your negative self-talk monster.
- You'll do your best to communicate honestly with your friends and family.
- You manage your time and space in a way that's productive and that suits you.
- You can be aware of when you're catastrophising and awfulising and know how to cool it down.
- Because you're human you'll sometimes screw up and get into conflict. It's how you deal with it that counts.

Now I'm cool I can help other people to be cool too!

# Glossary

**actions** Something that happens in the world around us that is outside your control. How you respond to an action is based on your beliefs, which affects your consequences.

**assertive** A way of being that is firm about who you are. Without being aggressive, it's a way of stating what your needs are and your ability to say 'no'.

**automatic thinking** The conversation you have with yourself that goes on in your head all the time. It's very important to become aware of automatic thinking in how it responds to actions in your life.

**awfulising** When you think about something happening in the future as being absolutely awful. It's about over-estimating how bad something might be if it happens.

**bad loop** A chain of events where negative beliefs create negative consequences. Those consequences make you believe your negative beliefs even more, creating a cycle that goes on over and over.

**behaviour** Things that you do in response to an action and your beliefs.

**beliefs** These are the things you believe about yourself, other people and the world. They affect the choices that you make, and therefore your behaviour and its consequences.

**black and white thinking** When your thinking leads you to believe that an event makes everything either totally good or totally awful (see also catastrophising and awfulising). Mostly, things have aspects of both.

**catastrophising** Similar to awfulising, where something happening in the future is predicted to be absolutely catastrophic. It is about over-estimating how totally destructive a future event may be.

**communication** The way in which information, thoughts or feelings are shared. Good communication is the key to good relationships.

**concepts** Ideas or theories about the way things work. Concepts are best understood first as ideas, and then put into practice.

**conflict** When two or more people disagree about something. At worst, conflict can end in a fight. At best, through good communication conflict is resolved.

**consent** Similar to permission, or saying, 'Okay, I agree'. In UK law, the age of consent for a sexual relationship is 16. This means that it is illegal to have intercourse before this age.

**consequences** These are the things that happen in the world as a result of the choices you make.

**core beliefs** These are the main beliefs you have about yourself and are usually very short sentences that feel true. They underlie your automatic thinking and your negative thinking, and are responsible for the way you see the world.

**cybershadow** This is the trail of information about you that can be found online. Because the information can stay up there forever, it is like a shadow that follows you around.

**emotions** These are feelings. By becoming aware of both your feelings and thoughts (and the difference between them) you can make better choices in your life.

**evidence** This is all of the information in the world that you can use to check your thinking and feeling to see if it's rational. Sometimes our beliefs make it so we don't pay so much attention to the evidence because of filtering.

**feelings** See emotions

**Feng Shui** A Chinese tradition of making your environment harmonious by the way you arrange your spaces and use objects such as plants and colours.

**filtering** When you take in some kinds of evidence but not others because it doesn't fit into your belief system. Filtering out good information about yourself leads to low self-image.

**gender** How masculine or feminine you feel in yourself, which can differ from the biological sex you were born with.

**good loop** A cycle of positivity where an action happens that creates positive self talk. These things combine to affect your behaviour, creating positive consequences that confirm your positive core belief.

**holistic** This is a perspective that takes the whole person into account. Looking after all aspects of your life including the mental, physical, emotional, spiritual and social realms.

**mental** All the stuff that goes on in your brain, including thinking and feeling.

**mindfulness** A gentle non-judgmental awareness of yourself. It can be calming, and helps you to observe and understand your thoughts and feelings.

**negative self-talk** A form of automatic self-talk (informed by your core beliefs) where you speak in a nasty judgmental way to yourself. It can lower your self-image.

**optimistic** A way of looking at the world that is generally positive in nature: where the glass is half full, instead of half empty. Opposite of pessimistic.

**oracle** A person who tells the future.

**peer pressure** When your mates put pressure on you to do stuff you shouldn't or don't want to do.

**perceptions** The way you see the world, like through rose- or crap-tinted glasses. Your perceptions are very important when it comes to the choices you make and how you feel.

**personality** The kind of person you are, what kind of character you have. Everybody has a different personality, and they should each be appreciated for being different.

**pessimistic** A way of looking at the world that is generally negative in nature: where the glass is half empty instead of half full. Opposite of optimistic.

**positive incentive** A reward for hard work, like a nice walk at the end of a hard day. It helps motivate you to get difficult stuff done.

**positive visualisation** This is when you close your eyes and imagine something positive in your future. By making the visualisation as clear and accurate as possible, you can improve your perceptions and feelings about an upcoming event (like an exam or presentation), making it more likely you'll have positive consequences.

**psychology** The science of human behaviour, thinking and emotion.

**self-image** The way you see yourself. It can be positive or negative and has a lot to do with your core beliefs.

**sexuality** How you express your intimate and sexual feelings and desires. It's about what kind of person you fancy (and what kind you don't); who you want to snuggle, kiss and fool around with.

**social** This is the world of all your relationships, friends, families, teachers etc. It's all the people in your life and how you and they make it all work.

**spiritual** This is beyond the physical, mental and emotional and includes all the big questions about why you are alive and what meaning life has. There are lots of ways to be spiritual, some people use religion, others do it their own way and others aren't spiritual at all.

**thoughts** This is all the stuff that goes on in your head like an internal conversation. A lot of our thoughts are informed by our core beliefs but we can change our thoughts by using evidence and through other exercises in this book.

**trust** Happens in relationships where you have a strong sense that you can rely on the other person and they can rely on you. It's one of the most important ingredients in good healthy relationships.

**vicious cycle** See bad loop

**virtuous cycle** See good loop

**Zen** A spiritual belief that comes from East Asia that teaches that meditation and awareness are the keys to a fulfilled life.

# Further resources

## General support and advice:

**ChildLine** is a confidential way to talk about your problems with a trained child counsellor. You can contact them online, ring, or email them and they are there to listen, whatever your problem.

Web: **www.childline.org.uk**

Phone: 0800 1111

**Get Connected** offers a free helpline service by phone, email or webchat for young people looking for support.

Web: **www.getconnected.org.uk**

Phone: 0808 808 4994

Email: help@getconnected.org.uk

**YoungMinds** is a charity that focuses on improving the emotional wellbeing of children and young people. Their website contains valuable information and advice on how to look after your mental health.

Web: **www.youngminds.org.uk**

Phone: 020 7336 8445

They also have a helpline to support parents: 0808 802 5544

**Youth Access** provides information on youth counselling.

Web: **www.youthaccess.org.uk**

Phone: 020 8772 9900

The **BBC** have a good advice website covering issues of emotional and physical well-being.

Web: **www.bbc.co.uk/radio1/advice**

## Sex and puberty:

**Brook** offers free confidential support and information about anything to do with sex, relationships and contraception.

Web: **www.brook.org**

**Books**
*A–Z of Growing Up, Puberty and Sex* by Lesley de Meza and Stephen De Silva (2013)

*Sex, Puberty and All That Stuff* by Jacqui Baily (Franklin Watts, 2005)

## Bullying:

**Beat Bullying** is a charity that works with children and young people across the UK to stop bullying.

web: **www.beatbullying.org**

**Cyber Mentors** is a website where you can get online support for bullying from other young people with bullying experience. You can also access online counselling.

Web: **www.cybermentors.org.uk**

## LGBT (lesbian, gay, bisexual and transgender) issues:

The **"It Gets Better Project"** was created to show young LGBT people who are having a tough time that you are not alone. It has loads of videos showing how folks got through the hard times they had as LGBT young people.

Web: **www.itgetsbetter.org**

**Terrence Higgins Trust** is an AIDS and HIV charity but they also have great information on different sexualities and safer sex. You can also get telephone support:

Web: **www.tht.org.uk**

## Thinking psychologically:

**Book**
*Think Good – Feel Good: A Cognitive Behaviour Therapy Workbook for Children and Young People* by Paul Stallard (Wiley-Blackwell, 2002)

## Yoga and mindfulness:

**Books**
*Yoga Pretzels: 50 Fun Yoga Exercises for Kids and Grown Ups* By Tara Gruber and Leah Kalish. (Barefoot Books, 2005)

*Planting Seeds: Practicing Mindfulness with Children* by Thich Nhat Han and Plum Village Community (Parallax Press, 2011)

# Index

## A

activities, after school 36, 44, 50–51, 57
asexual 63
assertive, being 68, 69
association 33, 46
attitude 42–43
awfulising 48, 76

## B

balance, life 12–13
beliefs, core 12, 15–17, 22, 25, 51
bisexual 63
body image 14
bullying 54–57, 64, 68

## C

catastrophising 48, 49, 74, 76
consent, age of 67
cyberbullying 58–59, 73
cybershadow 73
cycle, vicious 18
cycle, virtuous 19

## D

death, dealing with 38, 41
divorce, dealing with 38, 39, 40

## E

exams 6, 36, 44, 48–49, 70
externalisation 23, 34

## F

Facebook 47, 59, 70
families 26–31, 38–41
        conflicts 28–29
        dealing with big
        problems 38–41
        planning family time
        30–31
feelings, sexual 66–67
Feng Shui 32, 33
filtering 24–25
flirting 60–61
friendships 22, 41, 44, 45, 52–53, 60, 65, 68, 70–73

## G

gay 63, 65
gender 62–65
goals, achieving 74–75

## I

incentives, positive 37, 46, 47

## J

jar of coins 15, 24, 27, 50, 51, 55, 57, 76
journal, keeping a 10, 11, 13, 17, 23, 25, 26, 27, 33, 34, 36, 49, 76

## K

knowing yourself 10–13

## L

lesbian 63, 65
listening, active 28, 53
looking after yourself 12–13

## M

management, time 36–37, 70
meditation 6, 21, 33
mind reading 53
mindfulness 21

## N

networking, social 58, 70–73

## P

perceptions 6–9, 11, 16, 43, 46, 76
personality 11, 50, 51, 56
phones, mobile 47, 58, 59, 70, 71
pressure, peer 69
prophecies, self-fulfilling 18–19

## R

relationships, romantic 60–61
relaxation (exercise) 35
risks, taking 44–45

## S

safety, online 72
school (life) 14, 30, 42–51, 54, 56
school, starting 22, 43
self-esteem 9, 14, 56, 57
self-image 14–15, 25, 50, 51, 55, 76
self-talk 22–25, 39, 48, 57, 76
self-worth 14
separation 38, 40

## (continued)

sexuality 62–65
shyness, dealing with 52
skills,
        study 46–47
        timekeeping 36–37
sleep 33, 34–35
space, personal 32–33
space, study 33, 46
space, Zen 21, 33, 71
spider diagram 13, 51
Stanford Marshmallow
        Experiment 37
studying 46–47

## T

technology 58, 70–71
Temple of Delphi 10
thinking, automatic 20–25
timing 29, 53, 65
transgender 63

## V

visualisation, positive 49

## W

worries, dealing with 34–35, 46, 48–49

## Y

yoga 33, 71
YouTube 59